LANCE IN FRANCE

Six Years. Six Tours.
Six Victories.

A BRIEF HISTORY of BRILLIANCE

1999 TOUR DE FRANCE:

The Return of Lance Armstrong

The Highlights: After being diagnosed with cancer in 1996, Lance Armstrong returned to the French classic—he'd competed in one prior to being diagnosed, but had failed to finish—and demolished the field. The Texan won four stages, including one in the mountains, and every time trial. Armstrong described his victory to ESPN as "a fantastic story. This isn't Hollywood. This isn't Disneyland. It's a true story."

From the start, Armstrong was dominant, winning the opening prologue on July 3, 1999. In Stage 8, Armstrong retook the yellow jersey with a decisive win against the clock; with the mountain stages about to begin, Armstrong had already amassed a formidable lead of more than two minutes. In the mountains, the story was U.S. Postal, and the way they'd learned to support their team leader. By the time the Alps and Pyrenees ended, Armstrong had extended his lead to more than seven minutes. He won the final time trial—stage 19—and arrived victorious in Paris on July 25th.

In the Italian Alps, Lance is back.

The Final Analysis: The post-cancer Lance Armstrong was shown to be an entirely different kind of bike racer: physically lighter, and therefore better in the mountains, but also more patient, less inclined to spend his energy in impressive but ultimately inefficient bursts of speed.

The Skinny: This Tour began Armstrong's up-and-down relationship with the French press. There were whispers—and a few loud proclamations—that, given his medical history, Armstrong could not possibly have won without the use of illicit drugs. In fact, during the race, Armstrong did test positive for a corticosteroid—but the substance turned out to be a legal skin ointment.

The Teammates: The first U.S. professional cycling team to win a Tour de France was a star-studded group that included Tyler Hamilton, who finished 13th and was just beginning his long stint as the Texan's chief lieutenant.

Leader Lance poses with best climber Richard Virenque and best sprinter Erik Zabel.

The Rivals: Swiss rider Alex Zülle came in second, but even he admitted that "Armstrong deserved this race." The most notable Armstrong rivals were absent: Jan Ullrich, winner of the 1997 Tour, was out due to a knee injury, and Marco Pantani, the Italian climbing specialist who'd won in 1998, was serving a drug-related suspension.

2000 TOUR DE FRANCE:

The Doubters Are Silenced—Mostly.

Lance takes the City of Light.

The Highlights: Armstrong and his team remained low-key overall in the early stages of the 2000 Tour. Then they hit the Pyrenees, and the cycling machine that would become known as "The Blue Train" roared into action. In stage 10, at the base of the Hautcam—it was the fourth climb that day and the race would finish at the mountain's summit, 12 miles up—Armstrong attacked and Marco Pantani was unable to answer. Armstrong took the yellow jersey that day, but the race wasn't over. A few days later, Pantani and Armstrong dueled again, this time on the slopes of Mont Ventoux, the massive peak that rises out of the lowlands of southern France. In what he thought would be seen as a cordial gesture, Armstrong allowed Pantani to take the stage victory. The Italian rider considered the action insulting and, when the race reached the Alps,

Pantani punished Armstrong on the way up the
Courchevel, beating the Texan by 50 seconds and
taking the stage. But Armstrong's lead remained
intact, and the effort so exhausted Pantani that he
later quit the race. Armstrong iced his second
Tour de France *gateau* by winning the stage 19
time trial, taking his second yellow jersey into
Paris a day later.

**Taking
a time trial**

The Final Analysis: This is the capable
Lance Armstrong who would dominate cycling for
the next several years, winning with a combination
of masterly team tactics and impeccable personal
skills in bike racing's two primary disciplines:
climbing and racing against the clock.

The Skinny: Armstrong's only miscalculation
came on the 2000 Tour's final mountain, when the
Texan ran low on energy, allowing Jan Ullrich to
attack. The German rider gained nearly two
minutes on Armstrong, but it wasn't enough.

The late Marco Pantani sprints to a stage 12 victory over Lance.

Armstrong and teammates pose on the Champs-Élysées.

The Teammates: Once again, Tyler Hamilton was the second most dominant American, finishing in 26th place and working as the Texan's most dedicated supporter.

The Rivals: This was probably the toughest field Armstrong had competed against, with Ullrich at full-strength, an inspired and angry Pantani, and Spanish hot-shots Joseba Beloki and Roberto Heras both finishing in the top five. Armstrong would later neutralize Heras by hiring him for the Postal team.

2001 TOUR DE FRANCE:

The Master Strategist

The Highlights: There may be no moment more famous in recent Tour de France history than Lance Armstrong's successful attack on the legendary Alpe d'Huez climb during stage 10. One climb earlier, Armstrong had appeared to be in real trouble, looking deeply fatigued, slipping behind. Jan Ullrich's team, Telekom, took advantage of Armstrong's apparent weakness and pushed to the front of the pack, allowing Armstrong and his two Postal lieutenants, Roberto Heras and José Luis Rubiera, to rest a bit. By the time they reached the foot of Alpe d'Huez, with Ullrich dreaming of yellow, a refreshed Armstrong attacked. The "weakness" had been a brilliant ruse and Telekom had fallen for it completely. Armstrong powered up Alpe d'Huez at breakneck speed, humiliating Ullrich. As they neared the summit, the Texan glared back at his rival; the withering glance—since immortalized as "The Look"—utterly demoralized the German contender. Though there were still nearly two weeks of riding to go, and the Texan would face repeated attacks from Ullrich in the Pyrenees, Armstrong's hat trick was assured.

George Hincapie, Lance Armstrong, and Victor Hugo Peña going flat out.

The Final Analysis:

Armstrong's maturation was complete, and for the first time the possibility of winning five, or even a record six, Tours became a legitimate topic of discussion.

Lance in his second home, Paris

The Skinny: The criticism of Armstrong died down a bit in 2001. Could it have had something to do with Armstrong's decision to answer interview questions in French?

The Teammates: They worked for Lance; of the supporting Posties, Heras finished highest, 30 minutes back in fifteenth place. Hamilton, in his last year with Armstrong, was in ninety-fourth place. The highest ranking American other than Armstrong was Bobby Julich, racing for Credit Agricole. Julich, who was third in the 1998 Tour, finished in 18th position. In 2004, he'd win the Olympic bronze medal.

The Rivals: Would Jan Ullrich ever again win a Tour de France? Once more, the German came in second place, a position he'd continue to hold in every Tour he'd enter until 2004. Was it Ullrich's lack of fire? The conclusion most were reaching, and continue to reach, is that the German rider may, in fact, be more physically gifted than Armstrong, but he's just not passionate enough to win a race that is as much about the mind as the body.

2002 TOUR DE FRANCE:

All Lance, Almost All the Time

The Highlights: Armstrong described 2002 as "the year of the team," and never before had a single cycling squad worked with such clockwork unity and power, each rider dedicated to a single goal: getting "The Boss" to Paris in a *maillot jaune*. Rarely were any of Postal's rival teams able to put Armstrong under real pressure, and the Texan increased his lead day by day. The most exciting moments for Armstrong were his back-to-back mountain stage wins in the Pyrenees, but the true thrills came in the Tour's secondary battles: Richard Virenque, back after serving a drug suspension, unleashed a punishing attack to win the stage—and the hearts of his French fans—atop Mont Ventoux. And Australian Robbie McEwen won the sprinter's prize, finally upsetting six years of dominance by German powerhouse Erik Zabel.

The Final Analysis: Armstrong said it best in the post-race press conference: "I wanted to remember that cycling is a team sport. You need protection in the flats, and in the mountains. That security blanket makes a big difference. Some people talked about this team being the best in the history of cycling…. Give me these nine guys on the start line next year."

U.S. Postal, Bagnoles-de-l'Orne to Avranches, stage 7.

The Skinny:

Despite post-9/11 travel worries, thousands of U.S. fans made the trek to France to see and follow the Tour. If there were still catcalls about doping rumors, they were easily drowned out by flag-waving Americans, and by the end of the Tour, nearly every fan lining the course was won over by Armstrong's dominance. The Texan's fourth victory vaulted him past Greg LeMond as the winningest American in Tour history.

The peloton hair-pins at Saint-Maurice-Navacelles.

Lance in the ascendant

The Teammates: First among equals was

George Hincapie, the powerful, lanky rider who emerged as Armstrong's most important

supporter. Hincapie, a formidable racer in the single-day "classics" that led up to the Tour de France, was never far from Armstrong's side. But the entire Postal team was a well-oiled and well-conditioned machine. In the flats, Viatcheslav Ekimov pushed the team to faster and faster paces, and in the mountains, three diminutive climbers—Roberto Heras, José Luis "Chechu" Rubiera, and Victor Hugo Peña—kept their leader well supported.

The Rivals: After injuries and a drug scandal, Jan Ullrich sat out the 2002 Tour. Beloki finished second—seven minutes behind—and Lithuanian Raimondas Rumsas came in third. Rumsas was seen as a great hope for the future, but he became enmeshed in (yet another) drug controversy during the off-season, and never returned to form. Up-and-coming, however, was Italian Ivan Basso, who won the 2002 white jersey for the best young rider. Basso finished second in the 2004 Tour, and could be Armstrong's toughest rival in 2005.

Spain's Oscar Sevilla explains a fine point to best young rider Ivan Basso of Spain.

2003 TOUR DE FRANCE:

Only Human

The Highlights: From the outset, Armstrong looked less strong, less perfect, than he had in previous years. Armstrong faltered in the mountains, and for the first time in years his lead was counted in seconds, not minutes, by the time he reached the Pyrenees. The race was star-crossed in other ways: A crash in stage 2 broke Tyler Hamilton's collarbone, but the former Armstrong confidante, now riding as leader of Team CSC, continued and managed an astonishing and dramatic fourth-place finish. But the main event was the duel between Armstrong and Ullrich in the mountain region bordering France and Spain—one of the great sporting battles of all time. It had been set up by a time trial a few days earlier in which the German absolutely crushed Armstrong, cutting Armstrong's overall lead to 34 seconds. And in the Pyrenees, it looked as if Ullrich might close that gap—or at least keep the race undecided until the final time trial. However, as they climbed Luz Ardiden, luck intervened. Armstrong caught his handlebar on a spectator's purse and crashed. Even though the riders ahead, including Ullrich and Hamilton, followed Tour tradition and waited for Armstrong to recover, such a spill can often be demoralizing for a racer and destroy his rhythm and motivation. For Armstrong, it worked in reverse; he caught up to the pack, then pulled

Lance heads for the hills in the first mountain stage.

ahead and won at the mountaintop in front of tens of thousands of screaming fans. It was an astonishing moment, and it forced Ullrich to take desperate chances in a rainy stage 19 time trial. When he slipped and fell, the Tour was Armstrong's. He'd joined the elite club of five-time Tour winners.

Armstrong and peloton crossing a bridge near Gap, stage 9.

The Final Analysis: This was the 100th year of the French Classic, and it can reasonably be argued that there has never been a more thrill-packed edition of the event. "This," said Tour organizer Jean Marie LeBlanc, "is what this race is meant to be."

The Skinny: Though he finished formidably, Armstrong was a bit chagrined by his performance, and determined to do better: "I don't intend to be so vulnerable next year," Armstrong said, and it was a promise he kept.

The Rivals: Tyler Hamilton was a revelation; his courage and classy performance made him nearly as popular as Armstrong. Joseba Beloki was tragically cut down by a horrific crash in stage 9; the broken leg he suffered still hadn't fully healed by the 2004 Tour. And Jan Ullrich? Another second-place finish, but high expectations: "I'm getting closer," he said.

The Team: Though Armstrong seemed weaker, the Blue Train kept him in the running. In fact, if Postal hadn't won the team time trial in stage 4, Armstrong's final 61-second lead would not have been enough to earn him the yellow jersey.

2004 TOUR DE FRANCE:

A Rout en Route

The Highlights: From day one, Armstrong and Postal dominated. The biggest challenges the Texan faced, in fact, were staying dry during the Tour's rainy first week and staying away from crashes. His rivals seemed depleted from the start. Jan Ullrich finished the race in fourth place, and looked to be much worse than that until he battled back in the final week. The most exciting part of the Tour was the performance of French rookie Thomas Voeckler, who wore the yellow jersey for an astounding ten days, absolutely delighting the hometown crowds with his pluck and courage. This doubled the excitement for the French, as retiring climbing specialist Richard Virenque won a record seventh polka-dot climbing jersey.

Armstrong in the pack at Amiens

The Final Analysis:

Lance Armstrong emerged in 2004 as a full-on global star. Complete with a rock star girlfriend (Sheryl Crow), he became the greatest rider in Tour de France history (though his status as greatest rider, period, remains arguable: the Belgian Eddy Merckx, who had

five Tour wins, garnered far more individual victories, as well as the tours of Italy and Spain, during the 1960s and 1970s). But there's no doubt that Armstrong has changed cycling permanently—and forever transformed the sport in America, making it a major event rather than an elite and obscure European import.

Lance climbs to a mountain stage win in the Pyrenees.

The Skinny: In an effort to make the race more exciting, organizers packed the mountain stages late and close together, including an uphill time trial on Alpe d'Huez. But the backloading of the ascents made the early stages of the race rather placid, and the uphill push against the clock was so crowded and chaotic that it ended up feeling like a disruption rather than an innovation.

Lance makes a last stage adjustment outside Paris.

Library of Congress Cataloging-in-Publication Data is available.
ISBN-13: 978-0-7611-3798-6
ISBN-10: 0-7611-3798-X

Workman books are available at special discounts when purchased
in bulk for premiums and sales promotions as well as for
fund-raising or educational use. Special editions or book excerpts
can also be created to specification. For details, contact the
Special Sales Director at the address below.

Workman Publishing Company, Inc.
708 Broadway
New York, NY 10003-9555
www.workman.com

Printed in the U.S.A.
First printing March 2005
10 9 8 7 6 5 4 3 2 1

*O*nce again, in memory of Marco Pantani (1970–2004), winner of the 1998 Tour de France, an unlikely superstar who gave everything to the great race; a class climber, all sinew and speed; a proud competitor, who never thought of himself as anything but a potential champion; and a popular hero whose fans loved him without reservation, and who mourn him with great grief.

DEDICATION

BOB ROLL: To Robert G. and Lilla F. Roll, my dear if not doting parents, without whom my butt never would have seen the light of day.

DAN KOEPPEL: Thanks to the staff of Bicycling *and* Mountain Bike *magazines—past and present—for helping me live my Tour de France dream.*

ACKNOWLEDGMENTS

I'd like to acknowledge Mr. Dan Koeppel and Ms. Laurie Liss, without whom this book never would have seen the light of day.

In addition, thanks to Joe Lindsay; Rich Snodsmith and Marisa Gierlich-Burgin, and the staff of Backroads Bicycle Tours; Mark Riedy, Matt Philips, James Startt, Bill Strickland, and the staff of *Bicycling* and *Mountain Bike* magazines; Steve Malley, who commissioned the original "Tour de France A-Z" for *ESPN: The Magazine;* Chris DiStefano, at Shimano, USA; Zapata Espinoza, at Trek Bicycles; Rob Vandermark and Jennifer Miller at Seven Cycles; Warren Shumway, for his introduction to Tyler Hamilton; and Davis Phinney and Connie Carpenter-Phinney at bikecamp.com. Researching this book would have been impossible without two ready resources: the invaluable Tour de France statistics and history at Tom James's Veloarchive.com, and the most complete news accounts of the race (especially those written by Tim Maloney) at www.cyclingnews.com.

Finally, thanks to my terrific teammates at Workman: photo researcher Aaron Clendening, designers Paul Gamarello and Stephen Hughes, and editor Richard Rosen.

Contents

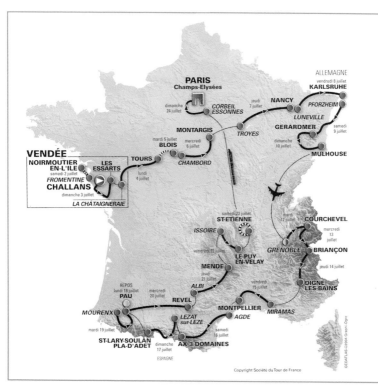

2005 Tour de France Crib Sheet

The best way to watch the Tour is to have a map of the event, as well as a profile chart (listing total elevation) for the climbing days. The map above is a good starting point; for more info, visit the official Tour de France Web site at www.letour.com (click on the British flag for English).

- Starts Saturday, July 2. Ends Sunday, July 24.
- Total distance 3,584 km: 21 stages
- 9 flat stages
- 3 mixed-terrain stages
- 6 mountain stages (three with mountaintop finishes)
- 2 individual time trials (TTs, 74 km total)
- 1 66-km team time trial
- 2 rest days
- 1 transfer by plane and 1 by train
- Total of 20 category 1, category 2, and "beyond category" *(hors categorie,* or HC) climbs
- 9 new stop-over towns: Fromentine, Noirmoutier-en-l'Ile, Les Essarts, La Châtaigneraie, Chambord, Gérardmer, Miramas, Agde, Lézat-sur-Lèze
- Total prizes: ε3 million with ε400,000 going to the winner

THE STAGES:

1   Saturday, July 2   19 km
    Fromentine–Noirmoutier-
    en-l'Ile (TT)

2   Sunday, July 3   182 km
    Challans–Les Essarts

3   Monday, July 4   208 km
    La Châtaigneraie–Tours

4   Tuesday, July 5   66 km
    Tours–Blois (team TT)

5   Wednesday, July 6   179 km
    Chambord–Montargis

6   Thursday, July 7   187 km
    Troyes–Nancy

7   Friday, July 8   225 km
    Lunéville–Karlsruhe

8   Saturday, July 9   235 km
    Pforzheim–Gérardmer

9   Sunday, July 10   170 km
    Gérardmer–Mulhouse

R   Monday, July 11
    Grenoble–Rest Day

10 Tuesday, July 12   192 km
    Grenoble–Courchevel

11 Wednesday, July 13   173 km
    Courchevel–Briançon

12 Thursday, July 14   187 km
    Briançon–Digne-les-Bains

13 Friday, July 15   162 km
    Miramas–Montpellier

14 Saturday, July 16   220 km
    Agde–Ax-3 Domaines

15 Sunday, July 17   205 km
    Lézat-sur-Lèze–Saint-Lary
    Soulan (Pla d'Adet)

R   Monday, July 18
    Pau–Rest Day

16 Tuesday, July 19   177 km
    Mourenx–Pau

17 Wednesday, July 20   239 km
    Pau–Revel

18 Thursday, July 21   189 km
    Albi–Mende

19 Friday, July 22   154 km
    Issoire–Le Puy-en-Velay

20 Saturday, July 23   55 km
    Saint-Etienne–
    Saint-Etienne (TT)

21 Sunday, July 24   160 km
    Corbeil-Essonnes–
    Paris, Champs-Élysées

TOTAL: 3,584 km

THE MAJOR CLIMBS:

Stage 9

Km 6.5	Col de Grosse Pierre	Ascent of 3.1 km at a 6.4% gradient
Km 22	Col des Feignes	Ascent of 9 km at a 2.9% gradient
Km 32.5	Col de Bramont	Ascent of 3.4 km at a 6.5% gradient
Km 64	Le Grand Ballon	Ascent of 21.9 km at a 3.6% gradient
Km 98	Col de Bussang	Ascent of 6.2 km at a 4.5% gradient
Km 115	Le Ballon d'Alsace	Ascent of 9.1 km at a 6.8% gradient

Stage 10

Km 118	Cormet de Roselend	Ascent of 20.1 km at a 6% gradient
Km 192	Courchevel	Ascent of 21.8 km at a 6.3% gradient

Stage 11

Km 55	Col de la Madeleine	Ascent of 25.4 km at a 6.1% gradient
Km 110	Col du Télégraphe	Ascent of 12 km at a 6.7% gradient
Km 133	Col du Galibier	Ascent of 17.5 km at a 6.9% gradient

Stage 12

Km 61	Côte des Demoiselles-coiffées	Ascent of 4.6 km at a 4.8% gradient
Km 88	Col Saint-Jean	Ascent of 13.2 km at a 4% gradient

Km 115.5	Col de Labouret	Ascent of 2.2 km at a 3.2% gradient
Km 156	Col du Corobin	Ascent of 12.4 km at a 4.5% gradient
Km 177	Col de l'Orme	Ascent of 2.7 km at a 3.9% gradient

Stage 14

| Km 190.5 | Port-de-Pailhères | Ascent of 15.2 km at an 8% gradient |
| Km 220 | Ax-3 Domaines | Ascent of 9.1 km at a 7.3% gradient |

Stage 15

Km 85	Col du Portet d'Aspet	Ascent of 2.7 km at an 8.4% gradient
Km 100.5	Col de Menté	Ascent of 7 km at an 8.1% gradient
Km 137.5	Col du Portillon	Ascent of 8.3 km at a 7.2% gradient
Km 162	Col de Peyresourde	Ascent of 13 km at a 6.9% gradient
Km 182.5	Col de Val Louron-Azet	Ascent of 7.5 km at a 7.9% gradient
Km 205	Saint-Lary Soulan (Pla d'Adet)	Ascent of 10.7 km at a 7.6% gradient

Stage 16

Km 51	Col d'Ichère	Ascent of 4.4 km at a 6.2% gradient
Km 71	Col de Marie-Blanque	Ascent of 9.3 km at a 7.7% gradient
Km 108.5	Col d'Aubisque	Ascent of 16.5 km at a 7% gradient
Km 118.5	Col du Soulor	Ascent of 2 km at a 5.5% gradient

THE 2005 TEAM DISCOVERY ROSTER

Of the racers below, nine will have been chosen by mid-June.

Name	Date of Birth	National Origin
Lance ARMSTRONG	9/18/71	United States
José AZEVEDO	9/19/73	Portugal
Michael BARRY	12/18/75	Canada
Manuel BELTRAN	5/28/71	Spain
Fumiyuki BEPPU	4/10/83	Japan
Volodymyr BILEKA	2/6/79	Ukraine
Janez BRAJKOVIC	12/18/83	Slovenia
Michael CREED	1/8/81	United States
Antonio CRUZ	10/31/71	United States
Tom DANIELSON	3/13/78	United States
Stijn DEVOLDER	8/29/79	Belgium
Viatcheslav EKIMOV	2/4/66	Russia
Roger HAMMOND	1/30/74	Great Britain
Ryder HESJEDAL	12/9/80	Canada
George HINCAPIE	6/29/73	United States
Leif HOSTE	7/17/77	Belgium
Benoit JOACHIM	1/14/76	Luxembourg
Jason McCARTNEY	9/3/73	United States
Patrick McCARTY	1/24/82	United States
Gennady MIKHAYLOV	2/8/74	Russia
Benjamin NOVAL	1/23/79	Spain
Pavel PADRNOS	12/17/70	Czech Republic
Yaroslav POPOVYCH	1/4/80	Ukraine
Hayden ROULSTON	1/10/81	New Zealand
José Luis RUBIERA	1/27/73	Spain
Paolo SAVOLDELLI	5/7/73	Italy
Jurgen VANDENBROECK	1/2/83	Belgium
Max VAN HEESWIJK	3/2/73	Netherlands

Foreword
By Dan Koeppel

A few winters ago, I became aware of Bob Roll's extraordinary ability to explain the Tour de France to *anyone.* I was visiting him in Durango, Colorado. It was snowy out, so we spent the day on what Bob called "hikes" in the hills surrounding town. I was relieved that I'd only be walking with Bob, because a bike ride with somebody who's raced the Tour de France four times feels something like being run over by a steamroller. However, I soon learned that Bob's idea of a promenade through the snow was *my* idea of how it must feel to be lost in the mountains in the middle of winter, with no food and on the brink of hypothermia. When we returned, I was completely, totally exhausted—in fact, I think necrosis had begun to set in—so Bob's suggestion that we visit a friend's house and watch Tour de France videos seemed perfect. I was a little curious, though, as the first tape started, about what's referred to as the audio portion: The sound was turned off.

Because Bob was going to tell us the real story.

For the next two hours, I heard what could only be described as a triple-threat combination of John Madden, Rex Reed, and a fire-breathing televangelist. Bob described what the racers were really feeling; he dished dirt about them; he shouted at them

when they appeared to be doing well and felt for them when they were suffering. On the big climbs, Bob filled in every excruciating blank: "They're turning themselves inside out," he'd say. When a normal English word didn't suffice, Bob's vocabulary underwent an instant lexicographical expansion: "He KREEGED hard!" Bob screamed after a group of sprinters, twisted in each other's wheels, slid to the ground in a bloody clatter.

I'd been obsessed with bikes, bike racing, and bike riding since I was six years old. I'd thrilled in 1989 when Greg LeMond won the closest Tour ever, and I was even happier that it was broadcast live, on network television, before an audience of millions. Of course, when I began racing, I discovered exactly how dismal my talents were—I just wasn't speedy—but I figured out how to earn a living by writing about bikes, by telling people how fast I wasn't. By the 1990s, I was doing most of my riding on mountain bikes, spending most of my weekends covering the burgeoning off-road racing scene in California and Colorado. Bob was racing mountain bikes by then, which was pretty incredible; hardly anyone has been able to manage a road, then an off-road, career as a professional bike racer. I knew Bob had raced the Tour de France for the legendary Motorola and 7-Eleven teams in the

1980s, and I made it a point to be introduced to him.

A lot of pro bike racers aren't terribly personable. Many are so focused on riding—they have to be—that they lack social skills; others just exist on such an elevated plane that you can't possibly hang out there with them—the air's too thin. Bob is different. He's one of the most engaging, funny, and do-it-my-way people you'll ever meet. I was in awe of him and, ever since, he's been my spiritual guide to the lore of bike racing, the art of wearing giant sideburns, and generally living large. Others agree: When Lance Armstrong began training after his battle with cancer, Bob was there. The future six-time winner of the Tour de France had asked Bob to help him train in the hills of North Carolina. Why Bob? I'm guessing it was because Lance knew that Bob would both give him a good workout and keep him laughing.

The era of Lance Armstrong has been nirvana for diehard bike racing fans. In 2001 the Outdoor Life Network began broadcasting the Tour de France live every summer, hiring Bob as a sort of wild-man commentator, a needed counterbalance to its authoritative but very British mainline announcers. As more and more people became Armstrong devotees—even folks who didn't care a bit about bikes—Bob's talents became more obvious. The reason he's almost certainly achieved more

fame as a television personality than he did as a bike rider is that, just as Lance Armstrong has figured out how to win the Tour as an American, so Bob has discovered how to explain the Tour as one.

In terms of general entertainment value, understanding, and fun, the Tour de France is absolutely accessible. The problem is snobbery. In the pre-Armstrong days, you often got the sense that the folks who really loved the Tour were the same ones who only listened to vinyl, considered donuts inferior to croissants, and would have been perfectly happy to own televisions tuned solely to PBS. Although they'd occasionally moan about the American public and its seeming rejection of pro cycling in favor of big-time, major league sports, I always got a sense—as Armstrong opened the sport to more and more people—that they were just slightly miffed that their little club was no longer as exclusive.

Bob Roll raced the Tour de France. As you read this book, you'll get a sense of what an achievement that is, and you'll understand that if anyone has the right to adopt a high-falutin' attitude, it's him. But he won't. He can't. Bob's brilliant in the way we all want to be: He's the kid who found his gift, found a way to use it, and ended up on the world stage. But Bob is doubly lucky, because after his first dream came true, a second gift appeared: the ability to lead regular folks like you and me into the joys, tragedies, and complexities of the world's most amazing sporting event.

A Fine Fast Madness

"The Tour de France is the greatest sporting event in the world."

—Ernest Hemingway, *The Sun Also Rises*

He was not polite. He was not hesitant. If he struggled, he certainly didn't show it—in contrast to the way his competitors fell, one by one, some brutally. The 2004 version of Lance Armstrong was many things: He was triumphant, winning a record sixth—and sixth straight—victory in the French classic. He was strategically brilliant, making months of pre-race reconnoitering and rehearsal pay off with perfect descents and end-of-stage sprints, turns that had not a drop of wasted movement, and prodigious climbs. He pedaled with so much unprecedented power and confidence that the punishment he meted out to his rivals was as much psychological as physical. Even veteran Tour watchers,

The Fab Five

Name	Tour Wins	Stage Wins	Jersey Wins Climbers	Sprint	Days in Yellow
Lance Armstrong	6	21	0	0	66
Miguel Indurain	5	12	0	0	60
Bernard Hinault	5	28	1	1	78
Eddy Merckx	5	34	2	3	96
Jacques Anquetil	5	16	0	0	51

True grit
Armstrong beats Basso to Plateau de Beille en route to his first stage win.

who like to think they've seen everything, were witnessing something new. If there's one word to describe Armstrong's performance in the first post-centennial Tour de France, it would have to

be: destructive. Armstrong destroyed the competition. He destroyed the mountains. He destroyed records. He destroyed time. He destroyed the illusion that he had no more illusions to destroy.

Before the 2004 Tour, every observer knew that if Armstrong won, his place among the greatest bike racers of all time would be assured. But whether he would actually head that list—especially above the Belgian Eddy Merckx, who won five Tours between 1969 and 1974, but also dominated other races the Texan has never entered—was debatable, with the Merckx camp holding a big advantage.

"Are you The Cannibal now?" a reporter asked Armstrong, referring to the nickname of the legendary Merckx.

Armstrong laughed. "I'm not *the* Cannibal."

That may be, but in 2004 he absolutely consumed his rivals—his hunger matched only by his lack of pity. The dominant theme in '04 was the Texan's unyielding mastery. The 2003 Tour was made of more mortal material; Armstrong faltered

He absolutely consumed his rivals— his hunger matched only by his lack of pity.

No strain, no gain
Armstrong leads Ullrich, in pink, up the Pyrenees.

**Mountain
madness**

Fans swarm an
Alpine switchback.

and the race was a cliff-hanger, thrill-packed to the very end.

In 2003, Armstrong seemed vulnerable enough to cast real doubt on a sixth victory. He finished strongly, but both Tour history and conventional wisdom suggest that difficulties in one Tour almost invariably foreshadow greater problems in the next. The event is so grueling that diminished performance has almost always indicated an irreversible decline. Anticipating 2004, Armstrong's rivals were licking their chops.

"He's showed us he's not invincible," said Jan Ullrich, the German who had finished second behind the Texan three times, and won the Tour on his own once. Other Americans—especially Tyler Hamilton, Armstrong's former lieutenant, who had toughed out the 2003 event with a broken collarbone, heroically finishing in fourth place—also had their eyes more squarely on the prize: "I'm riding to win," Hamilton said.

Besides history and age, there was another obstacle in Armstrong's way: the 2004 Tour's geography. Race organizers tweaked the 3,395-kilometer, twenty-one–stage route to be especially tough for Armstrong. They loaded the mountain stages toward the end of the race in order, they hoped, to keep the main contenders close until the grueling ascents began. And they added an unprecedented time trial—where riders battle against the clock, rather than each other—up Alpe d'Huez, the Tour's most legendary and painful ascent. Armstrong is one of the sport's finest climbers, but the reworked course added an element of uncertainty by putting the mountains even more in play.

Armstrong didn't complain and he didn't explain. As usual, he entered few races in the spring, preferring to train for the Tour on the

Tour route itself, a luxury not afforded cyclists riding for European teams, or most Americans, whose commercial sponsorship depends on good results over an eight-month season, rather than the single PR boost of a Tour de France win. While Ullrich whetted expectations by winning the Tour of Switzerland, one of Armstrong's few public outings was a disappointment: He struggled up Provence's Mont Ventoux during June's seven-day Dauphiné Libéré, a traditional Tour de France warm-up. The infamous peak had already vexed Armstrong during several Tours de France, and though it wasn't on the 2004 route, his troubles and his less-than-perfect form heartened the competition. (Not everyone, though; some, including Ullrich, argued that the Ventoux crack-up was a ruse. It would not be beyond Armstrong's skills as a strategist to attempt such a bluff.)

By the time the 91st Tour began in Belgium on the fourth of July, the bubble of anticipation had been inflated to epic proportions. America's excitement over Armstrong's attempt to win a sixth Tour only added to the madness. Some estimates put the number of U.S. visitors who traveled to France to see the event at over one million. Millions more, both longtime Tour fanatics and the newly addicted, settled in front of their televisions, where the Outdoor Life Network would preempt nearly every other program on its schedule, becoming an all-Tour, all-the-time broadcast. Speculation spiked, but of course no one knew for sure how it would turn out.

Except, perhaps, it now seems reasonable to say, Lance Armstrong.

The agony of the feet and other body parts—Frenchman Samuel Dumoulin crashes during the 8th stage.

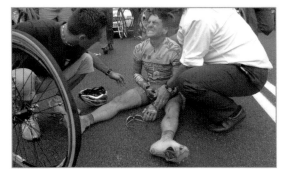

What Armstrong's victory lacked in cliff-hanging finishes, it made up as a virtuoso demonstration of his physical, emotional, and strategic genius. Not that it lacked the typically rich subplots that make the Tour de France the world's most dramatic sporting event. Fate played a role, especially, in vanquishing a few of the Texan's top rivals—and Armstrong's supporting cast, his U.S. Postal team, performed with clockwork brilliance.

The ebb and flow of the Tour de France usually means an initial week on the flats, followed by mountains, a few more days at lower altitudes, and then a decisive second run into the mountains. From there, the riders descend toward Paris, where the final drama is played out on the Champs-Élysées. This year's race was different. With the mountains loaded toward the end, some expected the initial stages to be rather low-key. They were wrong. Speeds were exceptionally high, and the sprint finishes that ended each day were brutal—and sometimes bloody. The biggest news of the early part of the Tour was during stage 3, when Spaniard Iban Mayo, who had been among the Texan's top rivals, crashed on a rough, cobblestone section of the route. (The course covered some of the same rutted roads as the legendary Paris–Roubaix single-day race—considered to be the hardest of the classic European cycling events.) Mayo lost nearly four minutes, as the first victim in a pattern that saw each of Armstrong's

Flat out on the flats

The early stages were unexpectedly fast, furious, and bloody.

top challengers fall by the wayside over the next two weeks.

In stage 4, Armstrong's U.S. Postal team dominated a rainy team time trial. That put the Texan briefly in yellow, but it was too early to make much of it; defending a Tour de France lead for that long is too exhausting, and everyone knew the real action would come in the mountains.

The next day, French rookie Thomas Voeckler gained the lead in a daring, 188-kilometer breakaway, sprinting away from the pack early. He stayed in yellow for the next two weeks, constantly battling back to the lead after being punished on sprints and climbs, and emerged as the Tour's most stirring new talent.

In stage 6, many of the top riders—including Tyler Hamilton—were caught in a dramatic pileup near the finish line, caused by just the lightest contact between two sprinters. Hamilton, the "other" American favorite, soldiered on over the next few days, but a personal tragedy demoralized him further: Hamilton's dog, Tugboat—a golden retriever who claimed the title of most famous pet in cycling, and who was almost as beloved as his master—was diagnosed with cancer as Hamilton competed. In 2003, as Hamilton winced his way to that legendary finish with a broken collarbone, Tugboat had stayed with his injured master every night after Hamilton's wife brought the dog from their home in Spain. This year, there would be neither a happy nor a heroic ending. Tugboat's cancer progressed quickly and he had to be put to sleep before stage 10. Hamilton abandoned the race three days later.

Over the next few stages, Thomas Voeckler was responsible for the most excitement. The

Frenchman Thomas Voeckler wore the yellow jersey for ten stages before he ran out of fuel.

A herd of cows and a herd of racers cross paths during the 11th stage, in central France.

French rider had taken the yellow jersey after stage 5 and now, as the race began to wind toward the hills, he struggled to keep it. Voeckler would attack, pedaling until he was exhausted, and then would fall behind, leaving most to believe his stint in the prized garment was over. However, each time Voeckler seemed about to fade, he would find hidden stores of energy—and rejoin the race leaders.

The entire middle of the Tour was filled with Gallic heroics. Frenchman Richard Virenque won stage 10—on Bastille Day—convincingly, with a huge breakaway. He would parlay that victory into his own ticket to the pantheon of Tour de France immortals: a record seventh polka dot jersey, the prize awarded to the event's best climber. Although not quite as appreciated as Armstrong's six wins in the general classification, seven polka dot jerseys confirmed Virenque, who had been disgraced several years earlier after a doping scandal and suspension, as his country's most beloved cyclist. The next day, the French continued to hold the spotlight as David Moncoutié won in the rolling hills of the Lot region of France, where his family comes from. "A stage win is great," the twenty-nine-year-old rider said, "but to do it at home . . . unbelievable!"

Once the race entered the Pyrenees in stage 12—the first true day in the mountains—it was a foregone conclusion that one of the top riders would take the yellow jersey from the valiant Voeckler. Armstrong was the best candidate, but Voeckler hung on for several more days as Armstrong whittled away his lead. Given Armstrong's faltering performance in the

Pyrenees in 2003, it was still an open question whether he'd be able to dominate. Armstrong quickly provided a piece of the answer. Stage 12's 164 kilometers included two of the Tour's most brutal climbs, the 12.5-kilometer ascent of the Col d'Aspin, and the slightly longer ride up Col du Tourmalet to a hilltop finish at the ski resort of La Mongie, where Armstrong had won two years earlier. Armstrong's Postal teammates—the "Blue Train"—paced their leader with beautiful precision, propelling him ahead of the pack; only Ivan Basso, one of Italy's best riders, kept up. The pace shattered Jan Ullrich, who fell several minutes behind, effectively putting the Tour victory he'd been hoping for out of reach. Basso outsprinted Armstrong at the finish line for the stage win. The Tour didn't yet belong to Armstrong, but the coronation was now close to inevitable.

The next day, stage 13, was nearly identical. More mountains, and more disappointment for the competition, with the exception of Basso. While Armstrong edged the Italian at the finish line, Iban Mayo—who had had a spectacular pre-Tour season, and entered the race as a favorite (and pedaled the Pyrenees with a home-team advantage, spurred on by thousands of Basque fans)—self-destructed. Emotionally spent, demoralized by his earlier crash, and perhaps exhausted by his grueling race schedule earlier in the season, he actually stopped midway and tried to quit. Mayo continued only because his teammates begged him to do so, and finished the stage fifteen minutes behind Armstrong. "It

Worthy of Monet
The Dutch Rabobank team makes an impression during the 14th stage.

Armstrong didn't need the stage victory, but he wanted it. "No gifts," Armstrong said afterwards.

Lance advance
Overall leader since the 15th stage, Armstrong and U.S. Postal descend the Glandon pass during the 17th.

was the worst day of my life," he said. It was typical Tour de France high drama.

Over the next six days, Armstrong's competitors gradually confronted their fate; they were battling, at best, for second place. Armstrong seemed absolutely determined to assert his own greatness. He did so most convincingly at stage 15's Alpe d'Huez time trial, an unprecedented ascent with an average gradient of 7.9 percent over 13.8 kilometers and twenty-one switchbacks, gaining over 914 meters. It was an insane day. Nearly one million fans crowded the road so tightly (some had arrived *two weeks* in advance) that race organizers later questioned one of the event's greatest traditions—the no-tickets, no-barriers, reach-out-and-touch-someone proximity of spectator and competitor. Armstrong himself said that the chaos created "a lot of fear" in him.

But he didn't show it. Armstrong climbed a minute faster than Jan Ullrich, who came in second; he beat Basso by more than two minutes. Armstrong's finishing time was just one second slower than the all-time record for Alpe d'Huez, set in 1997 by the late Marco Pantani, the Italian climbing specialist who won the Tour that year.

Armstrong won the next stage, 16, and the next, as well—helped in the Alpine climbs by

his team, which was functioning perfectly. And Armstrong did it with a verve that bordered on glee or viciousness (depending on who you asked). There was nothing modest about Armstrong as he crossed the finish line during his stage wins—he was pumped, grinning, and clearly having fun.

In the final, flatter stages of the 2004 Tour, Armstrong continued to dominate and intimidate. At the end of stage 17—the Tour's longest, at more than 200 kilometers, with five brutal Alpine climbs—German Andreas Klöden pulled ahead near the finish line. At this point, Armstrong didn't need the stage victory, but he wanted it, and reeled Klöden in over the last twenty meters, passing him at the last moment. "No gifts," Armstrong said afterwards.

The aggressive tactics continued in stage 18. By this time, Armstrong's victory was virtually assured—so the entire peloton was shocked when the Texan went after Italian rider Filippo Simeoni, who had joined a breakaway early in the race. Armstrong's presence in the front group doomed the breakaway—the other teams would be forced to respond—and Simeoni's effort dissolved. Why did Armstrong do it? Earlier in 2004, Simeoni had implied that Armstrong was taking drugs; Armstrong called him a liar, and Simeoni took him to court for slander (the suit is still pending; a decision will be rendered by the time of the 2005 Tour of Italy). After the stage, the Texan told the French media that he didn't think Simeoni deserved to win a Tour stage.

In the race's final time trial, stage 19, Armstrong again prevailed, taking his sixth stage win of the race. By then, barring accidents, his sixth win was assured.

Even before the race ended, as Armstrong rode toward Paris, speculation about the 2005 race abounded. Armstrong's longtime sponsor, the U.S.

Stars and stripes *toujours* American flags and fans saluted Lance Armstrong (third from left) daily.

Six!

Postal Service, has left the sport. The team is now underwritten by the Discovery Channel, a change in sponsorship that may affect Armstrong's decision whether or not to ride the 2005 Tour. Some sources have reported that Armstrong would prefer to attempt other events, such as the Tour of Italy or the individual hour distance record, that he has avoided in his relentless focus on the French classic. Armstrong is now thirty-four; he's already the oldest rider ever to win the Tour, and he has talked several times about retirement.

Despite that, the smart money—and this book—operates under the assumption that Armstrong will try for a seventh Tour de France victory in 2005. Armstrong's rivals will now spend the next few months wondering what they're going to do as well. Tyler Hamilton will likely not be there. After winning a gold medal in the Athens Olympics, Hamilton became embroiled in a scandal involving a positive test for an illicit blood transfusion; although America's favorite "nice guy" racer has strenuously denied the charges, he was dismissed by his sponsoring team, Switzerland's Phonak, in late November 2004; by the time you read this, the Union Cycliste International—the sport's governing body—will have determined whether or not Hamilton will be slapped with the mandatory two-year suspension. Regardless, without a team, it is unlikely that he'll be in the 2005 Tour de France. Jan Ullrich's chances are better. After his disappointment in the Pyrenees, the German battled back, finishing the 2004 Tour in fourth place.

At thirty years old, he's still got several good years in him. A head-to-head battle between the German and Ivan Basso, who ended up in third place, is among the most exciting prospects for the 2005 Tour.

In the wake of the Armstrong's victory, the biggest question of all keeps bobbing to the surface: Who is the fairest of them all? Besides Eddy Merckx, five-time winner Bernard Hinault deserves serious consideration, with twenty-eight stage wins to Armstrong's twenty-one, and seventy-eight days in yellow (Armstrong has sixty-six). Now, however, nobody who argues in favor of Armstrong can be dismissed.

"I don't know what to say right now," Armstrong said on the podium on July 25th. "It still has to sink in." He might have been tongue-tied, but with his girlfriend, rock star Sheryl Crow, on his arm, Armstrong no longer seemed like an American oddity in an esoteric, foreign event; he seemed like a global superstar.

Armstrong said his sixth victory was sweetest because it was so historic, and because it came after 2003's difficulties. More important, he said it was the most fun—"pure joy," he told reporters after the race. "It's as if I was with my friends and we were thirteen years old and we all had new bikes and we said: 'Okay, we're going to race.' It was like that for me this year. A simple pleasure."

Welcome to the Tour de France.

CHAPTER 1

C'est Le Tour

". . . the government could fall, and even the recipe for sauce béarnaise be lost, but if it happened during the Tour de France nobody would notice."

—Sportswriter Red Smith, covering the 1960 Tour for the *New York Herald Tribune*

If you're thinking of the Tour in terms of more familiar races, NASCAR or the Kentucky Derby or the Ironman triathlon, you might find the French classic a bit confusing. Keep two things in mind. The Tour is, in fact, many races, multiple dramas played out along miles of pavement, with many actors and many plotlines. The second thing to remember is the Tour's grandeur. This event is more beloved than the Super Bowl, longer than the Olympics, and more physically taxing than World Cup soccer. The Tour is also a living

The Tour: as French as berets and baguettes

symbol of the nation that hosts it. Because it has endured for so long, because it is so brutal, and because it traverses an entire nation, the race is the world's most involving sporting event. When you watch the Tour, there are no tickets, no sky-boxes, no stadiums. The action happens at a distance of inches. Racers know this proximity is a mark of respect. They're guests, however fleeting, in the towns they pedal through, and they return that deference as they pass. One of the emotions exchanged by fan and rider is gratitude. This unmatched intimacy between athlete and fan isn't one of the Tour's added attractions; the intimacy is the Tour's essence.

"Nous les sentons, ils nous sentent," one spectator said as he watched the final mountain stage: *We smell them. They smell us.*

The greatest gift riders offer the public is their suffering. This is quite different from the

Audience Participation:
A squirt of water is not always appreciated, but nearly always supplied.

relationship Americans have with our major athletes. For the most part, our stars are inaccessible and seemingly superhuman. Tour riders don't exist in a separate realm. It might be because they're doing something extraordinary on something so mundane (nearly everybody can ride a bike), or because the nearly feudal nature of the race itself condemns them to more familiar human circumstances. The control U.S. athletes have gained over their careers (and salaries) in recent years doesn't exist in the Tour. Until Lance Armstrong arrived, it was unthinkable for a Tour rider to cut his own major endorsement deals. Even now, only two or three of the best, most irreplaceable competitors can do so. The Tour is a working-class event. Those anonymous, middle-of-the-pack riders, whose labor is absolutely essential to any elite racer's chance of victory, can earn as little as $18,000 annually, although salaries at the Tour level for even support riders are often nearer to $180,000. The fans know this. The racers' toil mirrors their own.

The day-to-day intensity of the race provides a level of theater no single event can approach. As narrative, the Tour combines as many plotlines as an epic novel. The 2004 Tour's threads included Armstrong's attempt to win his sixth yellow jersey; the heroics of the young French star, Thomas Voeckler, who led the race for over a week; and the faltering performance of Armstrong's erstwhile nemesis, Jan Ullrich. There were personal tales, like the departure from the race of Tyler Hamilton, who was injured and heartbroken after the death of his beloved (and well-known) dog, Tugboat; and public ones, like the unprecedented throngs of spectators who crowded the roads climbing the legendary Alpe d'Huez—in an event cherished for the proximity it allows between public and participant, the scene was both elating and chaotic enough to be terrifying.

Wear yellow even one day and you'll never buy your own drinks in France for the rest of your life.

Every Tour is filled with measures of romance, scandal, heroism, crime, and punishment. There are years when the Tour's primary story is global—in the year 2000 the race celebrated unified Europe, dipping into four countries beyond France. The Tour can heal; in the late 1940s, after ceasing during World War II, the race became an expression of rebirth, a means of restoring a shattered continent (and not just symbolically: Wherever the Tour went, roads had to be repaved, villages had to be rebuilt). The first postwar Tours reminded people of the best things about their lives before; the race cauterized grief and made the future at last seem a possibility.

The Tour encompasses the full range of human emotion and much of human experience. Those things alone would elevate the event well above the ordinary. But the element of time—its sheer length—gives the Tour so many qualities of life itself. The Tour mirrors the inexorable, some-

Italy's Gino Bartali leads France's Apotre Lazarides on his way to a stage win in the Pyrenees in the 1948 Tour.

times grueling, and very mortal countdown we all face. Vince Lombardi would have hated the Tour because winning *isn't* everything; the race is about the work more than the *palmarès,* or triumphs. That hourglass can vex the weak and strong alike: One crash or flat tire, or a case of food poisoning, can destroy any chance of contending. There's a winner every day in the Tour—the rider who comes in fastest—but the clock doesn't set back to zero the next time out, as it does in other sports. Imagine if the World Series were played with the teams beginning each game with their cumulative run totals from the previous contests. In the tour, you can win five stages and still lose the race. And, as in everyday life, the Tour sometimes turns on the tiniest temporal fraction. In 1989 Greg LeMond started the Tour's final day nearly a minute behind—a margin most deemed impossible to overcome. But he outrode his rival, Laurent Fignon, eventually vanquishing him by a scant 8 seconds. After twenty-one days, all that separated them was the time it takes to cross the street. It was the closest margin of victory in Tour history. Fignon collapsed at the finish line, weeping. The loss haunts him every day. It wasn't LeMond who beat him: It was time, wielded in LeMond's hands.

Finally, there is romance. What else would you expect from France? Imagine a dream vacation to that country. You'd walk the Champs-Élysées, take a circuit around the Eiffel tower; you'd head south and meander through fields of sunflowers, moving on to the Alps and maybe the vineyards of Bordeaux. That's the Tour de France. Every year,

Greg LeMond, the first American to win the tour, puts the hammer down.

the race circles the country—lately, it has been clockwise in odd years, counterclockwise in even ones—hitting every Gallic note along the way. (France's hexagonal shape is extremely well suited for such a spherical setup; you couldn't begin to draw a circle in Italy or England.) Tour organizers make sure all of France is touched by the race. Although certain elements are present every year—the Alps, the final sprint into Paris—everything else comes, goes, and returns. For the nostalgically inclined, the Tour visits places where previous history was made. For those who look forward, there's always a new town or village,

16 Reasons Why the Tour de France Is Better Than the Super Bowl

1. The tailgate party lasts a month.
2. Admission is free.
3. More than 12 million people watch some part of the Tour in person, compared to roughly 80,000 who get to go to the Super Bowl.
4. Bike shorts are sexier than football pants.
5. The food is better.
6. So is the scenery.
7. Lance Armstrong is tougher than any football player.
8. So is Tyler Hamilton.
9. Men and their machines—no padding
10. And you're only inches from the action
11. Absolutely no Astroturf
12. Or end zone shenanigans
13. More struggle, more pain, more drama
14. The fans are crazier (and once you watch the Tour, you'll be one of them).
15. More Americans are kicking more butt in it every year.
16. Fewer big foam fingers

perhaps the next candidate for posterity.

The Tour has survived 100 years because it reinvents itself over time. Although, ironically, the race was initially sponsored by an automobile magazine, which sought to build interest in that still unfamiliar machine, the event was a testament to the greatest personal transportation device ever built—the bicycle. In the 1950s it embraced its inspirational postwar role. In the 1960s the event acquired jet-set allure. The Tour's biggest transformation came as the millennium approached, when the emergence of riders from countries never before represented—Australia, Colombia, Canada, and most notably, the U.S.—boosted its international flavor and appeal. Newcomers brought new strategies, new thinking: U.S. teams were the first to use sophisticated electronics to allow riders to communicate with each other. Greg LeMond's winning day in Paris was boosted by wind tunnel tests to determine the perfect aerodynamic position. American Tour riders arrived unencumbered by tradition, believing in sport more as a merit-based system than as a socially structured one. We might learn how to pedal smoothly in the pack, but we're always, on some level, outsiders. Only twenty-nine or so U.S. riders have participated in the Tour since Jonathan Boyer became the first to do so in 1981. Even now, the number of Americans in any year's event has never been more than ten.

Jonathan "Jock" Boyer, the first American to ride the Tour

But since 1986, when Greg LeMond became the first member of that tiny group to win the Tour, Americans have dominated, winning a nearly outlandish eight of the past eighteen tours. Those twenty-nine Americans make up less than 1 percent of the Tour's total ridership, but we've won almost 45 percent of the races.

As outsiders, we embrace the tenets of the Tour, but we feel a need to test its rituals, to reformulate them, to find out how they work. Lance Armstrong has won six Tours by combining sheer toughness with unprecedented analysis of exactly what it takes for *him* to win the race. He knows exactly what his body can and can't do; he knows exactly what each day will hold, because he's rehearsed it and broken it down countless times in the months before the race. That's how we, as American spectators, can watch the event—by finding our own intimacies with the riders who represent us. The tribute they pay us may not have the same seasoned meanings as what European riders give their fans, but it is tribute nonetheless. And our presence, either along the route or watching via satellite, returns the favor.

The Tour de France is a model of elegant design. It allows you to absorb its nuances at your own pace. The Tour rewards deepening study and appreciation, but there is no rush. You can learn its lessons organically, by just watching—and having fun from the start.

The event is the most regal of a royal family of bike races called grand tours. The two other major entrants into this category are the tour of Italy (the Giro d'Italia, held about six weeks before the Tour de France) and the Vuelta a España (the Spanish grand tour that runs after the French classic ends). The Tour de France combines both prestige (it was the first grand tour and has always been the one that most attracted the world's best bike racers) and geography (that unique, circular configuration—neither the Giro nor the Vuelta offers such well-ordered terrain). Until about two decades ago, many top cyclists rode two or three of the grand tours. Nobody has ever won all three in a single year, though Belgian Eddy Merckx, the winningest bike racer of all time, won the Italian and French races in 1970, 1972, and 1974 and added the Vuelta to his list of *palmarès* (racing honors) in 1973. These days, the Tour de France is so important and hotly contested that it is likely no rider can credibly hope to win it *and* one of the other grand tours in a single season. To attempt to do so would be to invite humiliation. In 2003 Italian Gilberto Simoni pedaled to victory in the Giro, and then boasted that he'd be the one to put Lance Armstrong to the test in France. Simoni finished more than two hours behind the Texan. Simoni is not that much less a rider than Armstrong, but the Tour is the Everest of cycling, and you can't top the world's highest mountain if you've exhausted yourself on a neighboring peak a few weeks before.

The greatest ever: Belgian Eddy Merckx

For the top contenders—and by extension their teams—the Tour is everything. You'll gain more fame finishing second or third in the Gallic classic than winning any of the other national races. With that in mind, here's a quick study guide to the Tour de France.

The Lay of the Land

The French sometimes refer to their beloved race as *la grand boucle,* "the big loop." I've mentioned the Tour's physical shape, but the concept is worth revisiting. The roundabout design of the Tour is enhanced by

The 1948 Tour
gets underway on
the Champs-
Élysées.

France's terrain distribution: The country's flat spots,
rolling hills, and pair of mountain ranges (the Alps
and the Pyrenees) are all the perfect distance from
one another, with Paris, the finish line, near the
center. This allows the Tour to unfold with splendid
dramatic tension: It starts in the lowlands, works up
the first mountain range, descends (giving riders a
needed respite—alongside utter dread of what they
know is coming), and then goes aloft once more
before the final drop into Paris. The Tour doesn't
follow a fixed course, though it almost always climbs
to key points, such as Alpe d'Huez, probably the
event's most legendary and feared mountain ascent.
Another special spot in the Tour is Mont Ventoux,
the only one of the race's legendary uphill torture
chambers that isn't in either of the big mountain
ranges. Ventoux, rising from the sunflower fields of
Provence, is a bleached, jutting hulk that has broken many top racers. The most visible race constant
is the ending in Paris, always with a high-speed
spectacle along the Champs-Élysées as the pack
makes speedy circuits through crowded streets,
until it finally finishes under the Arc de Triomphe.

The tour's geometric and geographical layout allows it to be much more than a simple race with a start and finish. Rather, the event ebbs and flows, following classic dramatic structure. In act one, the players sort themselves out and the main protagonists emerge. Act two, the week in the mountains, builds toward the climax. In the final act, the subplots resolve, and the story peaks as the riders pedal, if not into the sunset, then at least toward the Eiffel Tower.

The Object Though the basic dramatic structure of the Tour is as classic as any Greek tragedy, once the action starts, the race begins to look much more like a soap opera. The main storyline is, of course, the winning of the overall race—the "general classification," or GC. Winning the Tour de France isn't easy or simple, but the criterion for determining the victor is: time. After pedaling more than 3,000 kilometers in three weeks and climbing the equivalent of two Mount Everests, the person who did it fastest wins the

Miguel Indurain
climbs Alpe d'Huez.

yellow jersey. The margin can be close—in 2003, Lance Armstrong beat Jan Ullrich by 61 seconds, a time differential of seven hundredths of one percent over total in-saddle time of more than 80 hours. Or, it can be huge—in the very first Tour, Maurice Garin finished nearly three hours ahead of Lucien Pothier. That first race covered a slightly shorter version of the same route as the 100th-anniversary event, held last year—but, incredibly, the original riders covered the distance in just six tortured stages, some more than 36 hours long. The race was so intimidating that over the next decade, riders clamored for a softening of the rules that allowed no assistance and made the event into something resembling a forced march (you couldn't even accept a banana from an unauthorized spectator). Many racers were disqualified for cheating on the impossible distances, as additional stages—and kilometers—were added. The longest Tour was held in 1926, when Belgian Lucien Buysse won, pedaling 5,747 kilometers over seventeen stages.

Being the fastest isn't a matter of pedaling all out all the time. If a rider belongs to that exclusive category of potential GC winners, he has to strategize carefully, using his team, constantly trying to determine what rival contenders are up to. Because the race is so long, all efforts must be carefully measured: Give too much in a single stage, and a racer can "crack"—fall apart so badly that merely finishing becomes doubtful. Not everything can be solved by a good night's sleep.

The Tour's most punishing rule is the time limit: Every rider, every day, has to reach the *arrivée* (short for *ligne d'arrivée,* or finish line) within a fixed percentage of the leader's time. Nobody goes slowly—not even the shakiest, last-place rider. That fellow in last place—the French call him *la lanterne rouge,* or red lantern, after the light affixed to a train's caboose—is nevertheless one of the cream of the crop. The winners? They're the most elite of a spectacularly elite group. (Riders do drop out, but most struggle to finish the race as a matter of pride; almost every year between 80 and 90 percent of the 189–198 riders who started complete the event.)

Races Within Races

The fight for the yellow jersey is the Tour's raison d'être, but the competition is intricate and extends beyond the battle for that prize. Each day's action segments into minifights: long breakaways, in which a rider or two attempt to outrun the rest of the pack, pedaling all out—sometimes even nearing the finish line—before being pulled in by a pursuing (and far more aerodynamic) pack. The daily struggle for the stage win (the Tour breaks down into twenty stages, plus a short prologue stage, with a pair of rest and travel days mixed in) provides the drama of the GC battle in microcosm. For most riders, winning even one day of the Tour de France counts as the victory of a lifetime. Riders also compete for special jerseys: the *maillot vert* (green jersey) is awarded to the best sprinter; the *maillot à pois,* or polka-dot jersey, goes to the top climber; and the white jersey, the *maillot blanc,* is for the top young rider. The fights for the sprint and climbing jerseys are played out along designated stretches, sprint zones, or climbs categorized by difficulty, spread throughout each day's course. Each of these contests is a separate story that runs the length of the race. They wrap up together, in a sort of blockbuster ending, in Paris.

The Teams

The first official day of the Tour features the prologue, a short, ceremonial ride involving the twenty-one or twenty-two teams that have been selected by the Tour director

For most riders, winning even one day of the Tour de France counts as the victory of a lifetime.

The armada delivers: Lance Armstrong leads his U.S. Postal comrades in a team time trial.

through a fairly complex system of rankings, sponsor influence, and political considerations (for example, a lesser known French team may be added to the Tour and a worthier Italian team could be dropped; this is, after all, Europe). The teams start with nine riders apiece.

These aren't sports teams in the way American fans might understand them. They're not franchised or affiliated with a particular city or region; and there's no guarantee that any of them will be chosen to race in the Tour. Each pro cycling squad is sponsored by a company (or several companies) or organization looking for three weeks of solid publicity, which is provided by high-profile, two-wheeling, fast-moving, Lycra-clad billboards. The sponsors tend to be gigantic, even quasipublic, entities: lotteries, telephone companies, banks, or in the case of the only American squad to compete in the Tour during the last six years, the U.S. Postal Service.

In addition to the racers chosen for the Tour, every team has several other riders listed as alternates; competition between the team's twenty-five or so riders for one of the team's nine Tour roster spots can be fierce. Once the riders begin the French event, though, no substitutions are allowed, even if—as can happen—several team members drop out due to injury or fatigue. The squad also employs dozens of support staff, including doctors, mechanics, cooks, drivers, and masseurs, and it is run by a directeur sportif, almost always a former racer. You can get an idea of how pro cycling teams can sprawl at the minivillage set up at each day's finish line: A couple of luxury tour buses, along with a half dozen or more vehicles and at least fifty bikes, make the event seem more like a major rock concert than an athletic event.

The Players

So, what does everyone do? Let's look at the example of Lance Armstrong's 2004 U.S. Postal squad. (In 2005, the team's sponsorship has changed: It will be known as the Discovery Channel Pro Cycling Team.) One thing that might not be immediately obvious is that teams are constructed for differing purposes. A team like Postal/Discovery Channel centers around one rider, with the express goal of getting him into the yellow jersey. That kind of structure works only if a squad has a potential GC (general classification) winner—and not all do, because the Tour is so difficult that, in any given season, there are probably only four or five riders in the world capable of winning it. But the Tour is a multilayered event, and there's plenty of glory available, even for a team without a major superstar. A team not likely to field a contender for the overall victory usually concentrates on winning stages, which maximizes sponsor exposure. A good 2003 example of that was the Fdjeux.com

Lance and Le Tour Eiffel: Wish you were here.

squad, sponsored by the French national lottery. Nobody on the squad could realistically hope to finish in the overall top three, so the roster was packed with riders capable of maximum exposure despite that: Australians Brad McGee and Baden Cooke are both master sprinters; having two riders in the blue FdJ jerseys contending in explosive, high-speed (and very telegenic) finishes guaranteed plenty of air time. (All riders know that the jersey they wear is an advertisement; on most Tour days, the weather is so hot that riders pedal with the thin garment opened down to their belly button, but as soon as the finish line approaches, you'll see the potential stage winners zip up, to make sure their backers' logos are fully legible.)

A team like Discovery, of course, goes for the most coveted sponsor benefit: the overall win. Armstrong's team is an especially strong one, with racers who are fully capable of winning their own

big events—New Yorker George Hincapie is one
of the best single-day event racers in the world;
newcomer Italian Paolo Savoldelli won the 2002
Tour of Italy; another new face on Discovery is
Fumiyuki Beppu, a former Asian junior road champion, who will be the first-ever Japanese national
to race on a top-level Europe-circuit pro team.
Come July, though, everybody knows that they're
there for the Texan. A team that has a potential
yellow jersey winner has to be carefully picked.
Big, strong riders like Hincapie are needed to
power Armstrong through the flats; climbers, such
as the diminutive Portuguese, José Azevedo, are
there to help pull their leader up the hills. The
hardest-laboring of these riders are known as
domestiques, although the term doesn't exactly
mean what the English cognate implies. A *domestique* is more like an infantryman who supports a
team leader by dropping back for water, buffering
the wind, or chasing rival teams to tire them out.
(This was mostly my role during the five Tours I
raced, and it feels like three weeks of pulling your
brains out with tweezers.)

The most critical nonrider on the team is the
directeur sportif, or manager. The director rides
directly behind the pack, in a car groaning with
spare bikes, a mechanic, and tons of food and
drink. During a race, one of the *domestiques* usually drops back, stuffs the back pockets of his
jersey with these essentials—energy bars, maybe
a sandwich—and then pedals like crazy to the
front to deliver them. The team director's primary
job, as he sits in the passenger seat, is to plot
strategy. He's usually watching the race on television, and communicating with his riders by
wireless radio (look for the tiny earpiece each
racer wears). Every move made by a potential
rival is analyzed; split-second decisions on
whether that move has to be matched are made

and transmitted. Until the 1990s, information was relayed forward by *domestiques*; time differentials (how far ahead one rider was, or how much of a lead somebody had) were relayed via motorcycle, with a race official scrawling the information on a chalkboard that hung off the back. No matter how it is delivered, the combination of human skills and technical savvy is what makes a well-tuned squad. Such a team is key to victory, and also the key to one of the Tour's most fascinating paradoxes: It is a race won by individuals—but contested by groups.

The Race

The circular configuration of the Tour has remained unchanged since the beginning, but the scale has evolved. In the prewar era, the Tour was even more grueling, covering as many as 5,000 kilometers over as few as fifteen stages. In those days, the event was as much about finishing as about finishing fastest; it was a different kind of exercise in survival and beating the clock. Total distance began to decline in the 1950s, as speeds increased and riders no longer pedaled into the night. In 1919 Firmin Lambot won with an average speed of 24 kilometers (15 mi) per hour. The fastest-ever Tour de France was 2003, when Lance Armstrong's overall velocity reached 40 kph (25 mph). Today's format, averaging about 3,500 kilometers over twenty or twenty-one stages, emerged in the 1970s. Despite these differences, the overall rhythm of the Tour, so dictated by French topography, has remained much the same. Analyzing the 2005 route is a good way to understand the event's ebb, flow, and ultimate denouement.

The 2005 Race

Last year, Tour organizers attempted to make the race more difficult for Armstrong by loading the mountain stages and time trials (I'll explain these terms below) toward the end of the race. This followed Tour tradition of making the race as hard as possible for the favorite. "You need to prove you deserve to win," said five-time winner Bernard Hinault, who lost to Greg LeMond in the 1986 Tour. But the 2004 strategy backfired somewhat, because it slowed the action early on; the mountains *were* decisive, but Armstrong was so dominant that the hoped-for battles on the slopes never materialized.

This year, the Tour returns to a more traditional format, but with a few twists designed, once again, to make the race more competitive. The key word for this iteration of the Tour, according to Johan Bruyneel, team director for Discovery, is "balance." Bruyneel says the course is a good fit for Armstrong; one notable aspect of the 2005 race is how many different parts of France the course will traverse: more than 3,584 kilometers in 21 stages, the race will pass through thirty-nine of the country's departments (a regional designation similar to a province; France has ninety-five such areas). This will make the event as spectator-friendly as any Tour in recent memory, says race director Jean-Marie LeBlanc, "We have designed the 2005 Tour to focus on France, and we want to make it as easy for people to see as possible." Tour attendance topped two million last year; that number is expected to be at least equaled in 2005.

Day One—Paying Tribute In most Tours de France, the inaugural ride is called the prologue. This short race counts in terms of total time, but it is also considered a celebratory warm-up, a way to get the party started. This year, Tour organizers are skipping the prologue, opting instead for a short time trial—where racers compete against the clock, without the benefit of teammates, starting at two-

Eddy Merckx, the great Belgian cyclist, once likened racing to burning a book of matches: You've got only so many matches before you're out, so you have to pick your spots.

minute intervals and pedaling as hard and fast as they can to the finish line. There are three time trials in the 2005 tour, down from four in last year's race. Time trials can be critical. In 2003, eventual second-place finisher Jan Ullrich announced his return to form with a victory over Armstrong by a huge margin in the event's first time trial. The final against-the-clock contest in the 2003 Tour saw a reversal of fortune, as Ullrich crashed in the rain and Armstrong pedaled to victory. For 2005, the first time trial is just 19 kilometers—a distance racers can cover in less than thirty minutes. The course itself will be virtually flat, giving spectators a chance to watch cycling as an expression of pure, explosive leg power.

Week One—From the West The next seven days of racing are relatively flat—although in general this is a hillier tour than usual. Moving northeast from the Vendee region, on France's Atlantic coast, the race cuts across the entire country in a series of fast, long stages, moving

American Tyler Hamilton toughs it out with a broken collarbone in the 2003 Tour.

toward the German border. The Tour will dip into that country in stage 7, which finishes in the border town of Karlsruhe, where you can expect huge crowds to cheer on countryman Jan Ullrich (consistently Armstrong's most formidable rival) and his fanatically adored T-Mobile team, also based in Germany. Most of the days average more than 160 kilometers of riding, putting the men in the saddle for up to five hours. During the first week of the Tour, riders test one another, trying to gain time. These flatter stages are known for their dangerous, high-speed, and absolutely thrilling finishes. Sprint specialists—the thoroughbred racehorses of cycling—know that these stages are their primary chances to wear yellow. Sprinters are capable of explosive energy outputs over short distances: At the finish lines of these stages, dozens of riders will jockey for position, bumping and jostling one another, as they reach speeds of more than 80 kph (50 mph). Teams will try to place their riders right at the front, and then, as the finish line draws near, the fastest will catapult themselves forward, trying to lose their rivals. There may be no more exciting two minutes in the Tour than a sprint finish. There's certainly no more hazardous part of the race, in terms of the ability to do damage to a large number of riders: A crash in a sprint is a domino-effect clatter of metal and flesh, as riders collapse onto one another. In 2003 more than thirty riders went down during the second-stage sprint finish. American Tyler Hamilton broke his collarbone but went on to finish the race in fourth place, becoming a hero in the process. Another American contender, Levi Leipheimer, wasn't so lucky: He broke his hip in the pileup and had to withdraw (*abandon,* as the French say).

Another interesting aspect of the Tour's first week is the team time trial (TTT), which covers

The Ten Big Questions About Strategy (with Answers)

1. Since everyone competes individually, how is cycling a team sport?

The nine riders on a team have different duties: Some are climbers, who help their designated team leader keep pace in the mountains. Others are sprinters or stage specialists, who are on hand to win individual stages, which keeps the team in the news and money. The most common support rider is called a *domestique,* a French term meaning helper. *Domestiques* fetch water bottles and extra clothing from the team car and ride in front of the leader so he can draft (reduce wind drag). If a leader had to do all this work himself, he'd be too tired to respond to attacks.

2. So every team is gunning for the overall win, right?

Not necessarily. Not all teams hope for an overall podium finish, so they concentrate on other things: stage wins (via sprinters or breakaway specialists), or the jersey competitions. In fact, on any given day in the Tour, there can be up to five "races" happening: the overall, the day's stage, and the battles for the sprinter's, climber's, and young rider's jerseys.

3. What *is* the deal with the other jerseys?

The **green jersey,** also called the sprinter's jersey, is the points competition. Stage finishes carry points for first place to 20th place (on some stages), and there are often intermediate-sprint spots midway in the stage. At the end of the Tour, the rider who's amassed the most points wins the green jersey. Think of it as a consistency award. The garish **polka dot jersey** is the climber's prize. It works the same as the green jersey, but the points are awarded for categorized climbs; the number of points varies according to the difficulty of the climb. The **white jersey** is for the best young (under the age of twenty-five) rider. The Tour is such a hard race that young riders very rarely win the overall, so the white jersey is a way of identifying young talent, riders who might someday win the Tour.

4. What's happening in the sprint finishes?

You'll see three things. (1) Teams aiming for stage wins in the sprint set the pace very high in the final 30 or so kilometers of a stage. This discourages breakaways. (2) In the last few kilometers, riders from one or another team form a train, riding a team time trial of sorts. This is called a leadout. The riders take "pulls" at the front, riding as hard as they can before exhausting themselves. The idea is to put the team sprinter last in the train, where he won't have to see the front of the race (and face the wind) until the last 100 meters. (3) Riders jostle for position. Lesser sprinters often jockey to sit on the rear wheel of the favored sprinter, in hopes of using him to reduce wind drag (doing so is called getting a leadout) and then, using the energy saved by riding behind, slingshot to the front at the very last second. This jostling—at speeds up to 45 mph—makes sprint finishes very exciting and very dangerous.

5. Why isn't the winner the guy who wins the most stages?

Because the Tour is about overall accumulated time. A rider might, theoretically, win ten stages by one second each, but lose 10 minutes on one stage, so he'd be 9:50 down on overall time. It's rare for a rider to win the Tour without winning any stages, but it has happened.

6. Why doesn't a team leader have to chase down every attack?

The team leader chases only the riders who are threats for the GC.

Teams know in advance who the real contenders are, and they often pace one another until the big mountain stages, where real time gains are made. Other riders who attack are often let go to form a breakaway, because they will lose time in other stages and not be a threat to win the Tour.

7. Why don't riders simply attack from the start?

You can, and one rider, Jacky Durand, has made a career of winning stages this way. For the same reason you need teammates, though, it's almost impossible to win a Tour this way. A rider who attacks from the gun would have to set his own pace the entire way, fighting the whole peloton. Even if he's successful, he's still got to wake up the next day and ride hard again. A long solo break is just too tiring.

8. What's the most important thing for riders to do to ensure a good Tour ride?

Recover. The Tour de France is won in bed, goes one adage. After a stage, riders are immediately given some sort of sports drink, then taken to the team hotel for food and a massage. Dinner is followed by a short strategy session, or maybe a quick conversation with mechanics about needs for the next day's stage, and then it's off to bed. Tour riders burn between 5,000 and 9,000 calories a day during the four- to seven-hour stages, so recovery is the most crucial aspect.

9. So how do you win the race?

By marking your chief rivals and putting in attacks when they are most vulnerable. Eddy Merckx, the great Belgian cyclist, once likened racing to burning a book of matches: You've only got so many matches before you're out, so you have to pick your spots. Lance Armstrong uses his powerful team to lift the pace on climbs, saving him energy and insulating him against his chief rivals, and then attacking. He is also a formidable time trialist; in TTs, strategy matters little and significant time gains can be made.

10. What if you have to go the bathroom?

I thought you'd never ask. Often riders drift to the back of the peloton during the early, uneventful part of a stage. Large groups stop at the side of the road, and then pace back up to the pack. It's considered bad form to attack during un naturel, as relief stops are called on Tour radio. If a rider really has to go and things are popping at the front of the field, he can ride at the back and be pushed along by a teammate while he urinates to one side. Be careful not to draft him!

66 kilometers between Tours and Blois in stage 4. Although not every tour includes this tongue-twister of a contest, when it does occur, it can make a big difference. The team version of the event works just the way the individual time trial does, except that each nine-person squad leaves together. Everybody on the squad is given the same finishing time: that of the fifth rider across the line. The team time trial is fun to watch because it is an excellent example of how a pro cycling team works together. The strategic goal is to make sure the first five team members finish together, at top speed. This is done by getting the other four riders to pull their comrades forward, expending their energy, then dropping back into the rear positions, where their final times won't count. This is a delicate and difficult balancing

act, and the riders who do it well are showing the rest of the field that they're working as a unit.

Generally, the riders wearing yellow during the first week won't come near the tour's top final standings. These are days for individual glory through breakaways and attacks—and for those fast and savvy enough to win a stage, a small measure of immortality: Wear yellow even one day and you'll never buy your own drinks in France for the rest of your life.

Week Two—Going Up This is one of the most climbing-intensive Tours in recent memory. Stage 9, on Sunday, July 10, offers a preview of the mountains to come. The racers will make five ascents over the 170-kilometer route. But the most thrill-packed part of the day might be the descent into the finish-line village of Mulhouse: Riders will tear downhill at top speed over an astonishing 55 kilometers.

But the true mountains begin in stage 10, when the racers enter the Alps. These initial climbs could provide the first true glimpses of how the overall race might end. One thing you'll hear during mountain stages is talk about climb categories. Ascents are classified numerically, starting at four and counting down to one; the lower the number, the greater the difficulty. The most dreaded climbs are those that are considered

On the painful way to the Galibier pass in 1974's Tour.

hors catégorie—beyond category. The climbs are classified according to a formula based on length, steepness, and where during the stage the ascent appears. Some mountains that come early in one Tour are used as finishes in another, which often means a change in category, although the race's most infamous ascents are always in the unclassifiable realm.

Many of the Tour's make-or-break moments—for riders at the front, trying to win, as well as riders at the rear, struggling to stay in the race—occur on these slopes. Any of the major Tour climbs is exciting to watch (you've never seen such pain) but the most thrilling might be those that finish at a mountaintop. This is suffering and strategy at their most raw and brutal: in 2004, Lance Armstrong physically and mentally destroyed his rivals by pedaling away from them in the Alps and Pyrenees; unable to answer his attacks, his competitors became more and more demoralized, and understood that they were now battling, at best, for second place.

If there's a word to describe the four days the Tour will spend in the Alps in 2005, it has to be "classic." The most legendary and formidable ascents of the 103-year-old race are included. Stage 10 covers 192 kilometers, including the brutal 20-kilometer ascent up the Cormet de Roseland. Stage 11 follows one of the oldest and most fabled routes in the history of the Tour, with three climbs: the infamous Col de Madeleine, then Col du Télégraphe, and finally Col du Galibier, a 17.5-kilometer, sun-baked forced march that has destroyed Tour ambitions for many contending riders. Stage 13, with less climbing, should be a good day for last year's young sensation, Thomas Voeckler, to mount an attack.

Will the race have a clear leader by the final Alpine stage? Probably not, but there's almost

certain to be excitement—if any of the pre-race favorites has a bad day in the Alps, they'll very likely forfeit their chance for an overall Tour win.

The peloton hits Paris.

Week Three—Going More Up   This
year's Tour will likely be decided in the Pyrenees. Stages 14 and 15 look to be especially brutal—both are excessively long (220 and 205 kilometers, respectively) and both finish with climbs. Look for the race leaders to make big moves during the first of these two stages, especially on the final climb to Ax-3 Domaines.

Anyone simply hanging on to a high-level placement entering the Pyrenees should find himself shattered by the first day in that range. By the time the stage is over, the true leaders of the Tour de France will remain, and they'll be set to battle it out on the even tougher stage 15. This is, by far, the Tour's most brutal day: six massive climbs, the final quartet stacked in the second half of the day. Riders will be fighting one another on each climb, with feints and attempted breakaways; Team Discovery, with Armstrong's able, hard-climbing lieutenants, will be looking to dominate.

Many observers believe that the rider leading the Tour after stage 15 will be the one to take the yellow jersey all the way to Paris. This is possible, especially if the race is dominated by a single rider, as it was by Armstrong in 2004. But if the contenders are close, and remain that way for the final two days in the Pyrenees, the ride into Paris could turn out to be especially decisive.

And Finally, Paris and the Yellow Jersey
One day prior to arriving on the Champs Élysées, the Tour's last time trial takes place— 55 kilometers on a loop course in the town of Saint-Etienne. If the mountains haven't fully separated the men from the boys, this will be the Tour's decisive stage. The time trial is followed by the final race into Paris. This stage is usually ceremonial—the racers may even pass around a bottle of champagne—but if the time trial fails to determine a winner, even the last stage will be hotly contested. In either case, the last dash is thrill-packed: The racers circle Paris's landmarks ten times, passing streets lined with spectators; the final sprint runs the length of the city's most famous boulevard, finishing under the Arc de Triomphe.

It's almost impossible for an American fan to understand how much prestige the yellow jersey carries. It would be only a slight overstatement to say that the *maillot jaune* is a symbol of triumph in the hardest physical challenge humans have ever invented (at least in the realm of sports). Will Lance Armstrong be wearing that garment for an unprecedented *seventh* time? The odds, most observers say, are about fifty-fifty.

CHAPTER 2

A Century of Glorious Cruelty

"Through torrid afternoons, entire populations will present themselves before you, their hands raised in applause, their eyes wide open to catch a lasting memory of the battle."

—Henri Desgrange, founder of the Tour de France, speaking at the 1903 race

I ronically, the purpose of the first Tour de France was to promote a product that, though rather exotic at the time, would soon supplant the bicycle as the world's preferred marvel of personal transportation. It was called the automobile, and the Tour's first sponsor was a newspaper that covered motor sports.

Pedaling the Pyrenees in 1955

The race was the result of a hard-bitten newspaper war between *Le Vélo,* a daily journal dedicated to cycle sports, and Henri Desgrange's upstart publication, *L'Auto-Vélo.* Printed, respectively, on green and yellow paper, the publications had been playing a game of public one-upmanship, sponsoring spectacular bike races as a way to generate publicity and jack up sales, since competition-crazed fans lined up to buy the papers every morning to see how their favorite athletes performed. In 1902, Desgrange hatched an idea that seemed absolutely audacious: a bicycle race that would circle France.

The inaugural Tour de France wasn't as long as today's event; it covered 2,428 kilometers, compared to about 3,200 for modern races, though some early Tours would span more than twice the original distance. What made the race supremely difficult were the conditions under which it was run. This was Europe in the earliest days of the twentieth century. There were no paved highways. Muddy, rough dirt roads were actually a relief for the riders, because frequently the alternative was punishing cobblestone. In addition, the

1924 Tour de France winner, the ill–fated Ottavio Bottecchia of Italy, nears the summit of Col d'Izoard.

Teamwork: lighting up in the 1920s

bicycles had no gears. And the race would be divided into—this is the truly astonishing part— just *six* stages and held over eighteen days in July, taking into account that many of the stages would last more than a single day. Though he was a public relations genius, Desgrange wasn't being hyperbolic when he announced, in *L'Auto-Vélo*, the dawn of "the greatest cycle race in the world."

Black-and-white photographs of the early Tour give a sense that this was a quaint, old-timey event. Men in straw hats surround the riders, who wear knickers and turtlenecks; cigarettes—considered an athletic essential (they "opened the lungs")—are nearly always present. But the first Tour was nothing less than an exercise in out-and-out cruelty. Stages ran as long as 35 hours, through terrible weather—snow in the mountains, dust storms, vicious wind, and searing heat.

But there was also glory. After the sixty riders set out from Paris, they were greeted by larger and larger crowds. Desgrange's accounts of the race, distributed nationwide, tapped into an unprecedented mania for bikes. It was, after all, a golden age for bicycle design; to be a cycling

engineer was to be master of an elite technology
that attracted, and often required, genius—the sort
possessed by two American brothers and bicycle
builders named Wright. Desgrange was quick to
observe what would become the race's hallmark:
the symbiotic relationship between competitor
and spectator. "There were people everywhere,"
he wrote. "At windows, on rooftops, in trees, on
bicycles, in cars, on horseback, on foot. Never
before had such enthusiasm been seen." By the
time the first Tour de France returned to Paris, on
July 19th, the nation was in a frenzy. Tens of thousands of spectators crowded the streets to watch
twenty-one surviving racers led by tiny Maurice
Garin, nicknamed "the little chimney sweep."
Desgrange had a hit: "I have dreamed many sporting dreams in my life," he wrote, "but never have
I conceived anything as worthy as this reality."

Too Much Too Soon

When it was
not even two years old, the Tour de France almost
became a victim of its own success. The difficulty
of the event and the zeal it inspired, in both rider
and fan, threatened to uncork anarchy on the
course. In the second Tour, cheating was rampant:
Competitors were caught riding trains and hitch-
ing pulls on the back of motorcycles. Fans tried to
assist their favorites through sabotage. Nails were
found strewn in the road and, on more than one
occasion, near riots ensued as racers were chased
through towns by rock-throwing crowds. As if the
race weren't hard enough already, riders also had
to be entirely self-sufficient; they were forbidden
to accept help from anyone—even borrowing a
sweater could merit a penalty.

It was a mess, and when the race finally ended,
Desgrange was disgusted: "The Tour de France is
over," he wrote, "and its second celebration, I fear,
will also be its last. It will have been killed by its own

success, by the blind passions that it unleashed."
The honesty of the finishing riders was so questionable that the Union Vélocipédique—predecessor
organization to the Union Cycliste Internationale,
or UCI, the sport's current governing body—took
four months to announce the official winners. The
results were stunning: The first four riders were
disqualified, including Garin. The winner was
Frenchman Henri Cornet. It was a less than satisfy-
ing resolution for all concerned, but the race itself
survived and recovered. After just one year, and
despite the abuses, it had become so beloved that
it had to go on. Far from killing the Tour de France,
the passions Desgrange talked about had probably
saved it.

At the time, the United States was experiencing its own early bike craze. Track racing, often in
specially constructed cycling stadiums called velo-
dromes, drew crowds of up to 20,000. Top riders,
as well known as movie stars, would pedal for
as long as six days in arenas such as New York's
Madison Square Garden, which lent its name to
the endurance contests that became known as

Two Swiss racers take a pause that refreshes, and impress the local children.

Jacques Goddet, who had taken over management of the Tour alongside the aging Desgrange, stood up to the German occupiers, refusing to hold the Tour de France while his nation was not free.

"Madisons." The sport was one of the first to be integrated; one of the best-loved racers of that era was Marshall "Major" Taylor, an African American from Harlem who won the 1899 world sprint championship. The greatest of the early American racers was Frank Kramer, who won sixteen consecutive U.S. national championships, starting in 1901. At the height of his career, Kramer earned more than $20,000 annually, twice as much as Ty Cobb. Kramer even raced in Europe, with spectacular results: In two visits, he won thirty-one of the forty-three events, including the Grand Prix de Paris. He must have heard of the Tour de France. Did Kramer ever consider entering? Nobody knows the answer. Following the war, Kramer continued racing but never returned to Europe. It would be almost eighty years before another American rider would so profoundly dominate on those shores.

Meanwhile, in Europe, the Tour de France was evolving. More stages and distance were added, and the difficulty was increased, as well. The Pyrenees (where Lance Armstrong renewed his chances in 2003) became part of the race in 1910. The next year, Desgrange—not satisfied by the suffering he'd caused in France's southwestern hills—added the Alps. The Tour was suspended during World War I and resumed in 1919. That year Desgrange introduced the yellow jersey (it was the color of his newspaper's pages) to help the fans and officials keep track of the leader. Then, as now, the rider leading the overall classification at the end of each day took possession of the *maillot jaune*.

The Tour Goes To War

The Tour was a great source of French national pride that sometimes bubbled over into dismaying chaos. But as the 1930s came to an end, its potential to trans-

form the souls of those who loved it was beginning
to emerge. People were beginning to see cyclists
as symbols of their countries, as the living embodiment of human dignity and courage. The prologue
to this occurred in 1938, when Gino Bartali (the
deeply religious Italian champion, nicknamed
"Gino the Pious") won his first Tour with a spectacular breakaway on the Col d'Izoard, gaining a
full *17 minutes* on his closest competitor, Felicien
Vervaecke. (The strategy presaged the one used
by Lance Armstrong: Dominate in the hills, using
your strength to demoralize those you've sur-
passed, leaving them incapable of response even
when the event descends to flatter realms.) But
Bartali raced beneath the dark clouds of fascism
hanging over Europe. Mussolini, in control of Italy,
had sent one of his trusted generals to France to
"advise" the Italian sports director that a Bartali
win would be a great propaganda victory as well
for the fascist cause—which most Italians, including Bartali, then saw as a nationalistic movement
rather than the malevolent, disastrous force it
would become. Still, Bartali saw his Tour de France
victory as a win for all people, a demonstration
of courage and strength.

  In the 1939 Tour, Germany and Italy (the
Tour featured national, rather than sponsored,
teams in those years) did not compete. By the
next year France had been occupied. Jacques
Goddet, who had taken over management of the
Tour alongside the aging Desgrange, stood up
to the German occupiers, refusing to hold the
Tour de France while his nation was not free.
Goddet told them that the great bike race was
a symbol of peace, not war. His stance was heroic
and true to the spirit of the event, but it was not
enough to stem Desgrange's disappointment over
the symbolic destruction of his creation, which
was nothing if not a reflection of France. His

race gone, his nation overrun, a broken-hearted Desgrange died in 1940. A memorial to him stands at the summit of the Col du Galibier.

Bike racing continued during the war—the grand tour of Spain was held sporadically, the one-day Tour of Flanders classic in Belgium was held without a break, and "substitute" Tours were held in France—but these seemed more like the "fantasy" Tour, involving riders on paper only, that wartime newspapers published every July in an unsatisfactory attempt to sate the public appetite for *la Grande Boucle.* The real Tour de France stars were on the battlefield, including future winner Fausto Coppi (who spent much of the conflict as a prisoner of war in North Africa). After the war, *L'Auto* was gone; it had published under German rule and paid the price. In its place emerged a new sports paper,

Tragedies of the Tour

Death on the Tour de France is rare. Since the first edition, in 1903, only four riders have died (and in more than 100 years of competition, only twenty-eight riders have died in internationally sanctioned bicycling competition). The last Tour death was Italian Fabio Casartelli, the reigning Olympic champion, in 1995. Casartelli, racing for the U.S.'s Motorola team, was not wearing a helmet when he crashed into a concrete road barrier on the Col du Portet d'Aspet and died of head injuries. The race was neutralized the next day in his honor—the men rode noncompetitively, maintaining their places in the peloton—and two days later, a young teammate by the name of Lance Armstrong won the stage into Limoges on a solo breakaway. He pointed to the sky at the finish line and dedicated the win to his fallen teammate, saying that he had ridden with the strength of two men.

The first Tour fatality was Francisco Cepeda, who fell down a ravine in the 1935 edition, and the most notorious was the death of British rider Tom Simpson. The 1965 World Champion, Simpson was a strong hope for a podium finish in the Tour in 1967. On a day when temperatures topped 100 degrees, Simpson collapsed while chasing the leaders on Mont Ventoux. "Put me back on my bike," he said to a spectator, who grudgingly complied. Simpson wobbled a few hundred

called *L'Equipe (The Team)*, that remains, to this day, the best day-to-day reference a Tour de France fan can have—whether or not you can read French.

The great race did not return until 1947, when it was won by Jean Robic, an odd-looking, pugnacious rider who took the race in rather unspectacular fashion, without ever wearing the yellow jersey. It didn't matter. A Frenchman had won, and the Tour was back.

It took the next two years to restore the Tour's prewar legendary status. In 1948, an aging Gino Bartali returned. His exploits in the Giro d'Italia had already helped rebuild Italy—workmen paved the roads wherever he went—and now, at age thirty-four, he was hoping to provide an even bigger boost for his nation. Halfway through the race, the riders received news of a crisis: The

meters farther before collapsing again, this time for good. The official cause of death is listed as a heart attack, but his autopsy showed evidence of his having ingested amphetamines.

Drug use is endemic in cycling, but Simpson's amphetamine-related death forced the issue to the fore and led to the first modern drug-testing protocols in sports. Despite advances in testing, cheating continued. In the 1980s, the use of the red blood cell booster EPO was linked to the deaths, typically in their sleep, of more than twenty Dutch cyclists.

It wasn't until after Andrei Kivilev was killed in a crash at the 2003 Paris-to-Nice stage race that officials, after decades of trying, finally prevailed on the riders to wear helmets. Helmets are now mandatory in all races, but many riders despise them, and Tour de France racers are still allowed to throw them off at the beginning of the toughest climbs.

Injuries are common, although usually not severe ones. In 1960 Frenchman Roger Rivière fell and was paralyzed. He died fifteen years later, largely of crippling complications from the injury. Far more common are terrifying crashes from which the rider emerges miraculously unscathed. Case in point: In the 1951 Tour, during a descent in the Pyrenees, Dutch rider Wim van Est fell 60 meters down a ravine. His teammates, understandably, thought him dead, but van Est walked away unharmed.

chairman of Italy's powerful Communist party had been gravely wounded in an assassination attempt, and a general strike was called. Riots ensued and civil war loomed. The Italian prime minister himself phoned Bartali to make a simple request: "Win the Tour de France."

With any other rider such a demand might have seemed wishful thinking, but Bartali crushed the field in the Alps, and soon all of Italy was following the race. Political differences in Italy were put on hold or dissolved. An Italian was in yellow. On July 25 Bartali won his second Tour de France, a full decade after his first. The world had gone through hell in the interim, but Bartali's victory affirmed the capacity of the Tour de France to exalt the human spirit and even improve it. As crowds pressed closer to Bartali upon his return home, an overexcited director of the Italian sports federation exclaimed: "Don't touch him! He is a God!"

Raymond Poulidor celebrates a stage win in 1962.

Meanwhile, in America the rise of suburbia was giving birth to a car culture that reduced the bike's status to little more than a child's toy. But the Baby Boom was sowing the seeds of a new leisure lifestyle that would bring cycling back as a recreational hobby, which in turn allowed the most gifted riders to take up the sport as an athletic vocation.

By the 1960s the race had more than returned; it had become chic. A French rider named Jacques Anquetil —whose ego and good looks were fortunately matched by his skill and perfectionism—became the first rider

Five-time Tour winner Jacques Anquetil does a victory lap after number four, in 1963.

to win the Tour five times (1957 and 1961–64). Fashionable film directors made documentaries about the event (although it would not be until 2003 that the Tour was showcased in a feature-length animated film—the Oscar-nominated French movie *The Triplets of Belleville*). Movie stars now greeted the winners in Paris. However, the working-class heart of the race was still beating, pounding hardest in perennial also-ran Raymond Poulidor, one of the best loved of all the great French cyclists. Throughout the 1960s Poulidor raced—and finished just out of the yellow, reaching Paris in second or third place eight times, but never at the head of the pack. Anquetil beat him in a legendary duel in the Alps, but "Poupou" put up such a brave fight that he won the hearts of the fans. Poulidor raced hurt, bloodied, and infirm. He gave the event everything and, in doing so, became the event: He proved that the Tour isn't about winning, but about nobility, grace, and generosity of spirit. Poulidor's losses were due not to a lack of skill, but to timing. When Anquetil won his last Tour, in 1964, the way seemed clear at last for

Merckx takes the lead again.

Poupou to triumph. However, another rider, even more gifted than Anquetil, was arriving onstage to foil his ambitions.

Merckx The Great

Eddy Merckx is, quite simply, the greatest bike racer of all time. Know nothing about anyone else who's won the Tour and you'll get by—but you should know Merckx (his name rhymes with "works"). The Belgian's list of victories is staggering. He won the Tour and the Giro five times each. He won the Tour of Spain. And, three times, he won the world championship for cyclists, based on a single-day, annual event; winning it is similar to earning an Olympic gold medal. He broke the record for distance pedaled in an hour, covering 49.431 kilometers (30.7 miles). He won dozens of one-day classics, and thirty-four Tour stages (Lance Armstrong, by comparison, has taken twenty-one). Poulidor was no match, but he refused to give up, even managing his customary second-place finish spot in 1974, at age thirty-eight, behind Merckx in the last year Merckx won the yellow jersey.

Today's top riders concentrate on the Tour: Lance Armstrong knows that he can better tailor his training to win the Tour by riding his program, rather than pedaling early season races such as the Giro d'Italia, whose course may not be the most ideal for optimizing performance in July. Merckx just rode everything. He lived for victory, and winning wasn't possible in solo hours on the road. He had to compete. To do battle with Merckx was to be plunged into a world of pain. His 1969 breakaway on the Tourmalet may be the greatest single-day performance in the history of this race. With 130 kilometers to go, he took the lead, finishing 8 minutes ahead of his rival. Merckx's explanation: He'd heard that a teammate had agreed to move to a competing squad the following season and Merckx wanted to teach him a lesson. Yet Merckx was neither ungracious nor ignorant of the traditions of cycling. In 1971, to the astonishment of all, Spaniard Luis Ocaña was actually punishing the Belgian champion, leading

Eddy Merckx, nicknamed "The Cannibal," devoured the competition.

Poulidor raced hurt, bloodied, and infirm. He gave the event everything and, in doing so, became the event: He proved that the Tour isn't about winning; it's about nobility, grace, and generosity of spirit.

by 7 minutes into stage 14. While ascending the Pyrenees in the rain, though, Ocaña crashed badly. He was unable to continue, putting Merckx in the lead, but the Belgian champion refused to wear the yellow jersey the following day. "I won't claim a victory I didn't earn," he said.

Merckx attempted a sixth Tour win in 1975, as Armstrong will in 2004. Since the Belgian has been advising his Texan counterpart for several years, it goes without saying that Lance is aware of how difficult winning six times can be—and how, sometimes, even the most random things can get in the way. Merckx was leading as he climbed into the Alps that year, when a spectator emerged from the crowd and punched him in the kidney. Even injured, Merckx managed to finish the Tour and take second place. In 1976, a tired Merckx didn't enter the tour—although, unbelievably, coming in third place was Raymond Poulidor, then 40 years old.

The mid-1970s and early 1980s were a golden era for French riders. Bernard Thévenet won in 1975 and 1977, and in 1978 Bernard Hinault—a taut, aggressive rider whose nickname was "The Badger"—earned the first of his five yellow jerseys. Hinault's victories were interrupted by Frenchman Laurent Fignon, who took the race in 1983 and 1984 (and by Joop Zoetemelk in 1980).

French good fortune was soon interrupted by an unexpected development—the 1970s cycling boom in the United States. It was hardly a racing movement; mostly folks hitched saddlebags to their ten-speeds and toured around the country. The trend culminated in a mass bike ride across America, the Bikecentennial, to celebrate the nation's 200th birthday. Still, the interest in bike touring gave birth to a renewed fascination—at least for the ambitious few—with bike racing. Except for a brief stint in the 1930s by Joe

Magnani, in the 1970s George Mount and Mike Neel became the first Americans to ride professionally in Europe since the Frank Kramer era. In 1981 Jonathan Boyer became the first American to finish the Tour de France, in respectable 32nd place.

The Tour Goes Global

Canadians, Mexicans, and Colombians were joining the Americans. Another rider who joined Mount in Europe in 1981 was a skinny kid from Nevada, a former junior road champion named Greg LeMond. (LeMond had become interested in bike racing when, on seeing a group of riders speed by his house one morning, he said to himself, "I can go faster.") LeMond wasn't yet ready to race the Tour; he followed the classic pattern of top continental rookies, competing in (and winning) the 1982 Tour de l'Avenir (Race of the Future), a critical test for neophyte racers. LeMond followed that with major single-day race victories in 1982 and 1983. Finally, making the Tour his goal, LeMond moved to Belgium, to better "become European," as he told reporters.

In the annals of the Tour, Lance Armstrong's comeback from cancer is a huge and important story. It would be hard to argue that it isn't the race's greatest tale, at least on a purely personal level. But LeMond had his own comeback. After finishing third and second in the 1984 and 1985 Tours, respectively, LeMond fulfilled his destiny in 1986: He won the Tour (and invented the "Tour and nothing but the Tour" strategy that Armstrong now follows). Then, as he was preparing for the July 1987 race, LeMond was shot in a hunting accident. Like Armstrong, he nearly died; also like Armstrong, he had a difficult comeback. Unlike Armstrong, whose comeback has encompassed his entire postcancer career, LeMond's return seemed to have distilled into a single, thrilling day in

In 1998, riders quit to protest mandatory drug testing.

1989—probably the most exciting day the great race has ever seen. (See "Time Trial of the Century" on page 70.)

The first American champion would go on to win another Tour in 1990, but by 1991, suffering from the effects of shotgun pellets left in his heart lining, he'd begun the decline so many great Tour champions seem to experience. Once you lose, coming back is difficult. He finished seventh that year (to Miguel Indurain), the last five-time winner before Armstrong and the only one before Armstrong to take his five consecutively. In 1992 LeMond dropped out. Whether Greg would have won the two Tours he missed can never be known, but had he done so, he might have avoided the inevitable and invidious comparisons to a young, muscular former triathlete from Texas who slipped into the 1993 Tour and won a stage at age twenty-one. The era of Armstrong was about to begin.

Lance—a lot The modern Tour de France is alive and well. It survived scandal in 1998, when dozens of riders quit rather than submit to mandatory tests after drugs were found in the possession of one team trainer. (That year the race was won by a remarkable Italian climber, the late Marco Pantani.) If it can be said that the modern era of the Tour began with Lance Armstrong, then 1999 would probably be when the first chapter was written. Armstrong had left the pro circuit in 1996 after being diagnosed with cancer. He'd been given less than a 40 percent chance of surviving (some of his doctors later told him they'd been charitable even with that estimate) and told he'd certainly never race again.

He returned in 1998. He was a different person
—more focused, more aware of his gifts (and
blessings), more mature. He'd lost weight, become
leaner and faster. Though his results were at first
disheartening, there was little doubt that the
Texan now had the mind and body of a Tour
de France winner.

Armstrong entered the last tour of the millennium as one of the favorites (he'd had excellent
results all spring), despite lingering questions
about his health and unrelenting, cheeky speculation about whether his new physique was entirely
natural. Armstrong ignored the questions and
rode. He didn't disappoint. Like Merckx, he was
overpowering. He understood that, to win, he had
to hurt his opponents. "The trick to beating
Lance," one racer said, "is not getting him angry.
The problem is that if you try to beat him, he gets
angry." One of Armstrong's advantages, less
frequently mentioned, is his hardscrabble back-
ground. Born to a teenage mother and raised
without a father, Armstrong possesses a working-
class grit and hunger often lacking in better-heeled

**In this photo
finish** of the 16th
stage of the 1998
Tour de France, Jan
Ullrich beats Marco
Pantani.

U.S. riders, but present in nearly every
European champion. Armstrong dominated. He intimidated. In 2001
Armstrong hung behind rival Jan
Ullrich in the Alps, his face a mask of
pain. Commentators thought he was
finished. But as the riders turned
toward Alpe d'Huez (the stage would
finish at the summit), Armstrong
turned on the power. He pedaled past
Ullrich, shooting his rival a withering
glare. It had been a feint.

Nobody could beat him. Armstrong
won despite continued questions from
the press and hostility from many fans,
who felt he was too calculating, too

arrogant, and maybe too American. All that just made Lance madder. And madder meant faster.

Armstrong's victories through 2002 were beautiful to watch because of their perfection. He won by the same big margins, using the same overpowering style, supported by the same clockwork team and tactics. It won him plenty of fans in the United States—he won the way we like our heroes to win—but little goodwill in Europe. It took 2003 for the rest of the world to fall in love with him. For whatever reasons—personal problems (he separated from his wife after the race), physical difficulties, or the competition's having learned and adapted to his style—Armstrong looked vulnerable. He struggled. He suffered. Armstrong has always been human; he's always been a deeply emotional person. Now that humanity was finally on display, before millions. The 2003 Tour was won the way all the great Tours are won: through profound struggle and suffering. Armstrong's victory over cancer had possibly, in some ways, made his earlier victories seem too easy by contrast. In light of his fight for his life, to some it appeared that bike racing might be just a game to him. But as Bartali showed by winning after the war, as Poulidor showed by not winning at all, the Tour *is* a game, but one that always mimics life and, at its best, is indistinguishable from the currents that swirl in the world around it.

Ironically, in 2004, Armstrong's return to dominant form lost him a bit of that goodwill—but won him profound respect: "I don't like him," one French newspaper columnist snapped, "but he is the best ever."

CHAPTER 3

Not-So-Easy Riders

"Even a hard day's racing is never as long as a working day during harvest."

—RAYMOND POULIDOR, FRENCH FARM BOY AND BELOVED TOUR DE FRANCE ALSO-RAN

Your average Tour de France rider wouldn't turn any heads on the average beach, let alone on the set of *Baywatch*. The first impression he makes might be: "Wow. That dude is scrawny." Sure, you might notice that the guy has incredible legs, lean and rippling with muscle and smoothly shaved for faster healing when a crash scrapes them up. But upper body? Hardly any at all. Moreover, in the middle of racing season, the poor guy would be sporting one of the worst farmer's tans you've ever seen: arms and legs seared red, abruptly turning pale and pasty

Legs of Lance

During the twenty-one days of the Tour de France, the average racer uses a minimum of 6,500 calories a day, nearly triple the normal consumption for an average male. On the hardest day, that number jumps to 10,000— enough to burn more than three pounds of body fat.

where his shirt and tight-fitting shorts grip them. You might find it hard to believe that this person—who probably stands about 5 feet 8 inches and weighs less than 150 pounds—is a worthy competitor in the world's most difficult endurance event.

Until you went for a bike ride with him.

During the twenty-one days of the Tour de France, the average racer uses a minimum of 6,500 calories a day, nearly triple the normal consumption for an average male. On the hardest day, that number jumps to 10,000—enough to burn more than three pounds of body fat. Wim H. M. Saris, a sports physiology researcher from the Netherlands, told a writer for *The New Yorker* that the Tour is "without any doubt the most demanding athletic event. For one day, two days, sure, you may find something that expends more energy. But for three weeks? Never."

Look at the faces of the riders—all of them, from the leader of the peloton to the last finisher of the day—and you'll see faces that are haggard, almost brutalized. Because they spend so much time in the sun and so much time in aerobic debt—depleting the last stores of fat that remain in their bodies—typical bike racers mid-Tour look a lot like condemned men. French journalist Albert Londres, who had previously written about colonial penal colonies, witnessed the 1924 Tour and described the racers as *"les forçats de la route,"* or convicts of the road.

The Tour de France champion who most embodied this reality was probably Fausto Coppi, the great Italian racer and Gino Bartali's biggest rival following World War II. Whereas Bartali was movie-star handsome, Coppi, who'd grown up in the farming village of Castellania, south of Milan, had a nearly spectral appearance. Like Bartali, Coppi had been instrumental in restoring Italy's national pride in the dark years following the war, winning the Tour twice. There's a famous photograph of him just after his 1952 victory that indicates how joyless the physical aspects of such an achievement can be: The racer's face is cracked and darkened from exposure, his eyes stare downward, and he looks far older than his thirty-three years. Coppi's weathered appearance made him the working-class favorite in Italy. He epitomized tragedy. He'd been a sickly child who miraculously discovered God-given gifts when placed on a bicycle. He'd lost the best years of his career—six of them—as a World War II POW. And, following his retirement, he contracted malaria on an African vacation and died at the age of forty. His death was nearly as traumatic and personal to Italians as John F. Kennedy's 1963 assassination was to Americans.

The drawn look that Coppi was famous for can't be attributed to archaic training techniques and conditions, either. The look lives today. In 1998 it could be seen in the face of Marco Pantani, the Italian climber whom many fans saw as the reincarnation of his star-crossed predecessor, as

The late, great Marco Pantani, 1998 winner and climber extraordinaire

When Armstrong's lung capacity was measured at the Cooper Institute, a top study center for exercise physiology, it ranked highest of any athlete the researchers had ever studied.

he ascended Les Deux Alpes, the sister climb of Alpe d'Huez, rising from the same valley and just a few kilometers down the road. Pantani was on his way to victory, but he looked as if he was taking a vicious beating. In the 2003 Tour Tyler Hamilton wore a similar look, made worse by the constant pain of his injuries. As for Armstrong, suffering was rarely etched on his face. The 2003 race changed that. A newspaper image of a team official helping Armstrong off his bike following his turning-point triumph on Luz-Ardiden depicts a champion who has spent every ounce of energy he had. In victory, the Texan looks as if he's been through, and lost, a war.

To understand the Tour de France rider's body, I turn to Lance Armstrong, not only because he's the most recent superstar of the Tour de France, but because he's also one of the most examined and physically understood athletes of all time. Armstrong has a scientific bent—he believes that knowing the way his body works gives him an edge—and his experience with cancer makes him a natural laboratory specimen.

Anyone can tell the physical difference between an athlete such as Armstrong and a professional basketball or football player. Bike racers tend to be built more like runners, though cyclists are often considerably smaller. Bike racers who *win* the big races are also physically distinct from those who compete in shorter events or possess the various terrain-specific specialties of successful Tour de France team members. Armstrong is bigger than most of the pure climbers, the lightweight *grimpeurs* who can produce large amounts of energy for extended periods, and whose lack of bulk makes best use of that increased power output. He is rangier than the sprinters, who have tremendous leg-muscle mass,

which consists primarily of the fast-twitch fibers capable of producing explosive results in short bursts.

How does a rider get the body he needs? Genetics play a huge role. Aerobic exercise requires, as the term suggests, oxygen; oxygen is the fuel your muscles use to propel you forward. The oxygen is delivered to the muscles by blood. So, one of the first gifts a champion cyclist has to have is the ability to take in a lot of oxygen. This is commonly referred to as lung capacity, and Lance Armstrong's is prodigious. He can absorb more oxygen per breath than almost anyone on earth—more than the vast majority of his two-wheeling compatriots and almost twice as much as the average male. When Armstrong's lung capacity was measured at the Cooper Institute, a top study center for exercise physiology, it ranked highest of any athlete the researchers had ever studied.

All that oxygen means better-working muscles. But at some point—a hard sprint to the finish line, say, or one of those painful climbs—even the

Don't try this at home: Thierry Marie, now a French television commentator, in 1995

Time Trial of the Century

On the morning of July 23, 1989, the only man who believed Greg LeMond could win the Tour de France was Greg LeMond. It had been a difficult year of some ups but more downs, but Greg was solidly in second place on the last day of the Tour. For most men, that would be enough.

There were just 24.5 kilometers to ride to Paris, in an individual time trial. LeMond, in second place overall, would have to make up 50 seconds on leader Laurent Fignon—impossible, given that the stage was too short, the mostly downhill course too easy, and LeMond's deficit too great.

But LeMond had a plan. He calculated that, on a normal day, on this course, he could take maybe 30 seconds out of Fignon. Not enough. Still, with some new equipment, he might squeeze those precious extra 20 seconds out of the situation.

Earlier in the race, LeMond had experimented with a pair of aerodynamic handlebars. They put him in a skier's tuck, dramatically reducing his drag. He had used them to win the race's first individual time trial. Fignon had tried them too, but declined to use them in the race.

As Boone Lennon, the Idaho-based ski coach who invented the bars, fastened them to the bike, LeMond pulled up hard on the bars to test them. They gave; they needed to be tighter. Lennon, famously, fashioned a shim out of a Coke can to hold the bars steady. LeMond also added an aerodynamic helmet from

LeMond's triumph

greatest athlete exhausts his genetic capacity for oxygen. You've probably experienced the feeling yourself: pain manifested as a burning in the legs and lungs. When your muscles aren't getting enough oxygen, your body relies instead on lactic acid, which it produces as a result of the anaerobic exertion. To oversimplify, the lactic acid helps act as a stand-in for oxygen when your muscles are worked to the extreme. Two factors come into play

Giro, designed to fit sleekly along his back when he was in the aerodynamic tuck on his new bars.

He told his team director not to give him any time splits; he would simply ride as hard as he could during the time trial, and that must be enough. Fignon, riding without aero bars, his trademark ponytail flapping in the breeze, left the start house in Versailles two minutes after LeMond, almost assured of his third Tour victory and a great day for France.

Almost from the start, LeMond gained time. Fignon's director, the legendary Cyril Guimard, shouted to Fignon from the team car at the 5-km mark that he'd already lost 10 seconds. Fignon lifted his pace. By the 10-km mark he'd lost 19 seconds. Impossible! At the 18-km mark, with just 6.5 km to go, Fignon had lost 35 seconds. Suddenly he was in a desperate fight for his title.

Onto the famed Champs-Élysées, LeMond rode like a freight train, stormed down the cobbled street, and flashed across the finish line in 26 minutes, 57 seconds. His average speed of 54.4 kph (33.8 mph) still stands as the fastest Tour time trial in history.

Fignon clawed at the road, his face a rictus of pain and panic. On the final straight, he pounded toward the finish while the clock ticked away precious seconds. A spellbound crowd watched: 27:47, 27:48. Still Fignon pedaled, crossing the finish line at 27:55—8 seconds too late. He collapsed from his bike, falling into an aide's arms only to be told, "Laurent, you lost the race."

Greg pumped a fist in the air and hugged his wife, Kathy, as the mob enveloped him. From the controversy of his 1986 win over teammate Bernard Hinault, his nearly fatal hunting accident the next year, and his struggles to return to racing, LeMond had traveled the long road back to win the most exciting Tour ever with the ride of the century.

when athletes enter this physical state: first, how much lactic acid their muscles produce; second, how quickly those quantities are disposed of. Armstrong has a double strength. His body creates less lactic acid, and gets rid of it faster, than most people do. This is ideal for bike racing, especially in the mountains and for the sustained effort required by the time trials—the two disciplines that most often determine who will win the Tour de France.

All the genetics in the world can't help a rider who is suffering from even the most minor affliction. It could be a distracting personal situation, or the pressures of sponsorship or team politics. It could be a meal that didn't sit right.

Armstrong has other genetic gifts. His heart is about 30 percent larger than the average person's. His resting pulse is 32 beats per minute—less than half what a normal, fit adult might register. This combination means Armstrong is capable of high levels of exertion, sustained far beyond the point at which ordinary mortals hit the red line of exhaustion and collapse. Even Armstrong's bones are superior: His femurs, the driveshafts of pedaling, are freakishly long, relative to the rest of his leg. If all this sounds like the Tour de France champion is one in a billion . . . well, yes. That's why hardly anyone can do it—and why a lot of folks just don't understand what it takes.

Even Armstrong's illness has contributed to his success, and not just in psychic terms. Armstrong had great potential and won plenty of big races before he was diagnosed with cancer; but whether he would have gone on to win the Tour is an open question. His body was different then, heavier. The 20 pounds he shed during chemotherapy (a process so radical that it permanently alters the body) have stayed off. Armstrong frequently talks about this change, and the psychological one: that his life-and-death struggle remade him physically and mentally. It sculpted him, a contender with potential, into the perfect Tour de France specimen.

Iron Wills and Iron Curtains

What about the other racers? Jan Ullrich, whom many see as another example of a "perfect" cycling specimen, looks quite different from his American rival. Both men are large for the sport—Ullrich is one of the peloton's rare 6-footers. The German, however, is two inches taller than Armstrong and, at 160 pounds weighs about 10 pounds less than the American. (By contrast, the smallest rider in the 2004 Tour was the

Russian Alexandre Botcharov, of the Credit
Agricole team, at 5 feet 5 inches and 119 pounds.)
Ullrich's height gives him greater mechanical
power than Armstrong, and his lighter weight
should be an advantage, as well. Both men possess an astonishing ability to take in oxygen
(Ullrich's measured oxygen capacity is, in fact,
a hair higher than Armstrong's). The Texan does
outshine his rival in terms of maximum power
output, but Ullrich edges Armstrong when the
ability to produce sustained power is measured.

In short, these guys are both virtually superhuman. So, why does Armstrong win and Ullrich
come in second (four times) or fourth, as he did
last year? The answer may lie in nurture (or lack
of it), not nature. Jan Ullrich was discovered
in East Germany at age four; he was a product
of the vanished communist country's regimented
sports machine, which chose and trained talent
with ruthless efficiency. When the Berlin Wall
fell, a changed world offered Ullrich astonishing
opportunities. He became a wealthy and celebrated star and was subject to a slew of
distractions that his upbringing had denied
him. While Lance Armstrong was enduring his
cancer ordeal, Ullrich was on a very different
odyssey: He was experiencing freedom—both
the good and the bad of it—for the first time.
He partied. He crashed cars. Most of all, he failed
to train in the winter, arriving at the Tour a little
heavy, a little less prepared. That's not the way
you get to wear the yellow jersey in Paris. In fact,
Ullrich was so widely regarded as an example of
squandered potential that most cycling insiders
had written him off by 2003. His long-time team,
Telekom, let him go; the 1997 Tour winner
signed with the Bianchi squad and returned to
Telekom only after his formidable performance
in the 2003 race.

Because they spend so much time in the sun and so much time in aerobic debt, depleting the last stores of fat that remain in their bodies, typical bike racers mid-Tour look a lot like a condemned man.

But 2004 was a disappointment for Ullrich, who said as the race started that he had a strategy for beating Armstrong, and that it was simply a matter of who would mentally dominate. Ullrich planned to take advantage of Armstrong's only (and rather slight, it must be said) weakness: his emotions. Armstrong rides best when he's angry, full of aggression. Ullrich's more calculating temperament should have made it possible for him to stay under the Texan's radar, sticking close and waiting for the right moment. But it didn't work. Instead, Ullrich weakened, faltering in key stages, and only gaining strength toward the end of the race. He seemed to lack the desire to win—proof again that riders pass the trying physical tests of the Tour not just with the bodies they've been given, but also with the mental discipline they've developed.

CHAPTER 4

Of Bikes and Men

"Isn't it better to triumph by the strength of your muscles than by the artifice of a derailleur? We are getting soft. . . . As for me, give me a fixed gear!"

—HENRI DESGRANGE, IN *L'AUTO-VÉLO*, 1902

The bicycle that today's Tour de France competitors ride is an oddly paradoxical machine. On the one hand, it is a miracle of modern technology, benefitting from materials and fabrication methods—titanium, carbon fiber, computerized machining of parts—that were unheard of just a decade or two ago. Modern Tour bikes are designed for maximum efficiency and perfectly balanced strength, to provide all-day durability; stiffness, for responsive

The most advanced and specialized equipment is used for time trials.

acceleration; and flexibility, to soothe road shock. They have aerodynamic wheels with bladed spokes; twenty speeds (with shifting that positively clicks each gear into place); and pedals that lock the feet to the bike, as ski bindings do, so that not an ounce of power is wasted as riders hammer uphill. Many of these innovations are fairly recent, and they've pushed the price of a pro bike toward the stratosphere: $5,000 gets you in the door—barely. Ride one and you're sure to be awed by the nimble—jumpy, for those not used to it—way the bike handles. Lift one and you'll be even more amazed: A Tour de France bike tips the scales at a mere 16 pounds or so, the weight of a bowling ball.

So, by the numbers, the earliest Tour de France bikes seem like prehistoric beasts. They weighed much more, were made of steel, and had one gear. On the other hand, put Lance Armstrong's Trek Madone, the bike he rode in the 2004 Tour, alongside the French-built Automoto that Henri Pélissier rode to victory in 1923, and you'll find they have a lot more in common than that both machines got their riders to the top of the Galibier. The two wheels are the same. The chain-and-cog drivetrain is the same. The curved handlebars, stretched-out rider position, and leather saddle, all basically the same. Yes, if you were to find a mint-condition Automoto and place it alongside the Trek, you'd be able to see the difference— but what you'd be noticing is the contrast between siblings, not an ancient paterfamilias and his distant descendant.

The one huge difference between the two bikes is gearing. Until 1937 Tour de France bikes were restricted, for the most part, to just one gear. That meant struggling up the hills and powering through the sprints on pure muscle—without the mechanical advantage offered by today's finely

tuned, varied terrain-loving drivetrains. At most, the earliest Tour bikes had two gears: a small cog on one side of the back wheel for going faster, and a slightly larger one for climbing. The climbing cog was freewheeling and worked the way today's bikes do: When you stopped pedaling, the cog stopped moving and the bike coasted. The smaller cog, however, was fixed; if the rider stopped pedaling, the bike would stop, too—abruptly. Early Tour de France riders had to keep their legs moving all the time in the small cog. If they wanted to change, they had to stop, remove the back wheel, and flip it around. It was a tedious process—though it did allow photographers to get good shots of the briefly stopped racers, which is why the wheel flip is the subject of so many old Tour images.

Nearly all bikes sold today—and every bike ridden by professional road racers—uses a derailleur to shift both front and rear gears. The derailleurs lift the chain up and down a cluster of cogs—ten in the rear, two in the front ($10 \times 2 = 20$; if you have a mountain bike, which needs a broader range of gearing, you're likely running nine by

Early Tour competitors chose between just two gears, and had to stop and flip the rear wheel around to change from one to the other.

A forest of bikes on team cars, ready to be called to action

three, for a total of twenty-seven speeds. The ten-speed you grew up with ran five by two). Though a few derailleurlike shifting systems were tried just after the turn of the century, they weren't allowed in the Tour de France. The race then was a tightly regulated affair, and it still is. The idea was to prevent technological innovation from leapfrogging physical skills; the Tour was, as Desgrange said, a test of muscles, not artifice. (Technologies banned today include certain kinds of aerodynamic handlebars and bikes that are so light that they'd have to be considered disposable, good for a day or two of racing but not much else.)

The derailleur that most recreational cyclists would recognize, and the one that came to dominate the Tour de France for nearly fifty years, was invented, in legendary fashion, by a young Italian racer named Tullio Campagnolo. Competing in one of Italy's late-season races, high in the Dolomites, Campagnolo was struggling up the snow-covered roads of the Croce d'Aune pass, when he stopped to undertake the tedious process of flipping his wheel. In those days, that meant unscrewing a pair of large wing nuts, turning the wheel, and refastening and tightening it, all by hand. Campagnolo was so cold he was unable to free the wheel. At that moment, the future bike parts innovator shouted five legendary words: *Bisogno cambia qualcosa de drio!* Something back there must change!

Campagnolo's first invention was the quick release, the ubiquitous levers that unlock a bicycle's front and back wheel and are found, in basically the same form, on nearly every bike sold today. Campagnolo soon realized, however, that removing the wheel easily was good—but not having to remove it at all would be better. In 1933 he introduced a system that used a series of levers and rods to push the chain up and down a cluster of cogs. At the same time, a French company, Simplex, was working on a competing design that used steel cables, rather than rods, to shift the chain up and down. It was the Simplex design that was first allowed in, and used to win, the Tour de France in 1937.

Yet it was Tullio Campagnolo who became a legend in cycling as important and powerful as Eddy Merckx. In 1948, Gino Bartali won the Tour with a Campagnolo derailleur design that was truly revolutionary, a complex and beautifully crafted piece of equipment with a major improvement: It was designed as a pivoting parallelogram, allowing the chain always to remain the same distance from the cog set and always at uniform tension. This eliminated the jamming and throwing problems that limited the use of earlier shifting systems to only the most daring and ambitious riders. Campagnolo's 1950 update was even more important: The Gran Sport rear derailleur came with a matching front changer; the ten-speed had been born. The basic Campagnolo design remained

When a rider has a problem, "a mechanical," as it's called, a team car with a roof rack full of spares pulls up alongside and a quick swap is made.

The Bike's Murky Birth

Like many inventions of the industrial age, there's a bit of debate over how the bicycle was invented, and by whom. Some folks say that Leonardo da Vinci made a drawing of a bikelike device in 1493; others claim that the sketch is a hoax. Another potential bike inventor is France's Comte de Sivrac, who many believe created a wheeled propulsion device in 1791. But that may be a hoax, as well. A better candidate might be the team of Meyer and Guilment, whose cog-driven, pedal-powered machine is now on display in the Paris Musée des Arts et Métiers. The problem is that nobody is sure whether the device actually was created in 1868, as claimed. What is certain is that by the late nineteenth century, many inventors were applying themselves to the problem of two-wheeled transit. Scotsman Kirkpatrick Macmillan built a machine that had rear-wheel drive and front-wheel steering in 1845; others added pneumatic tires, brakes, and wheels with spokes. One candidate for maker of the first bike that really *looked* like the bikes we ride today is Englishman John Kemp Starley, who introduced his "Safety" design in 1885. Bike historians have argued about the "true" inventor—there are plenty of other suspects—for decades, and they continue to do so. The rest of us can just watch the Tour and be grateful to them all.

unchanged for nearly four decades, and bikes equipped with Campagnolo components utterly dominated the Tour de France. Though a few other component companies managed to find their way to winning bikes in the 1950s, by the next decade the Italian factory had virtually locked itself to the yellow jersey. Starting in

1968, Campagnolo won twenty-eight of the thirty-one Tours. (After U.S. enthusiasts began hearing about the Italian company in the 1960s, having a "Campy"-equipped, lightweight racing machine was the ultimate bike geek's dream.) A few other companies did win an occasional Tour de France (in 1989, Greg LeMond used French parts), but Campy was utterly dominant.

Until 1999, that is, and Lance Armstrong. It makes sense that the rider who defied every expectation, who did everything his way, would break from tradition when it came to equipment. But the Texan's decision to use a Japanese drive-train on each of his U.S.-built, Tour-winning bikes has a surprising origin: The parts on Armstrong's bike got there because of the ordinary American's penchant for fun.

A U.S. Postal team mechanic—a "wrench"—prepares for race day.

American Revolutions Even as
serious bike enthusiasts in the U.S. were coveting Campy in the 1970s, the less well heeled were finding perfectly good alternatives: efficient, low-priced,

Spare bikes and wise counsel are never far behind.

and light shifting systems from Japan's Sun Tour and Shimano. Another popular derailleur brand, Simplex (the original Tour de France shifting system) featured a plastic changer found mostly on French Peugeot bikes. They worked beautifully until they self-destructed, usually within a year or so. Shimano, especially, worked hard to build a high-quality suite of racing parts, and in 1973 introduced the Dura-Ace group as a direct competitor to Campagnolo's Record system. The Flandria team created a minor scandal in Europe when they used the "foreign" product in the 1973 Tour de France and managed a stage victory.

One big difference between Greg LeMond and Lance Armstrong is the origin of their hardware: LeMond, for the most part, rode European-built and -equipped bikes. Armstrong rides an American-made frame equipped with Japanese parts. For LeMond, there were few options: Through the 1980s the dominance of European (and especially Italian) bikes and bike parts remained basically unchallenged; it was part of the legendary tradition of fine craftsmanship that made everything bike-related from the European factories—frames, saddles, handlebars, and clothing, along with parts—the most desired, the most expensive, and the best. But something was happening in the U.S. that would change all that: Far from the cobblestones and mountains of Europe, some iconoclastic U.S. riders were taking their bikes off-road, equipping them with fat tires and motorcycle-style handlebars. The craze started in northern California in the early 1970s, and by the end of the next decade the mountain-bike boom was in full swing.

Japanese parts makers responded quickly, coming up with durable and easy-to-use components for off-road cyclists. Campagnolo failed to respond: It came out with a half-hearted mountain component group that showed little of the company's legendary functionality and innovation. As more and more riders began pedaling off-road, Shimano's reputation grew and grew. By the early 1990s the technological innovations of the Dura-Ace group, which drew inspiration from the company's dirt-bike offerings, plunged Campagnolo into serious trouble. It looked as though the company might go the way of dozens of other continental parts makers, joining Simplex as a brand name remembered only by collectors and classicists.

It didn't happen. Campagnolo roared back in the early 1990s. It abandoned mountain biking and concentrated on making the best road-bike parts in the world. The company will never be as dominant as it once was, but the "Dura-Ace versus Campy Record" debate is one of the most heated and partisan disputes of the past five years. Lance Armstrong, riding as an iconoclast, has given Shimano advocates plenty of ammunition in recent years, and in 2003 all the Tour de France champion's jerseys—Armstrong's yellow, along with the green and polka-dotted jerseys—were won by Shimano for the first time. In 2004, the Italian and Japanese component makers again shared the podium, with Lance Armstrong riding a prototype version of the Dura-Ace drivetrain that is only now becoming available to consumers.

Minor adjustments, such as resetting saddle height, are done on the fly.

The rise of innovators from around the world isn't limited to bike parts: The 2004 Tour saw bikes manufactured in Italy, France, three brands from the United States, and frames built in Canada, Switzerland, and Spain; the lightest bikes in the Tour, ridden by the Spanish ONCE (pronounced "own-say") team, came from Taiwan.

Bike Talk

Bikes are pretty simple, right? Two wheels, frame, gears, and brakes. But look again: The bike of a Tour racer is about as far removed from most people's rides as Michael Schumacher's Formula One Ferrari is from your Ford. Here's a look "under the hood" at what makes a Tour bike special.

Frame: To maximize power transfer from the drive train, frames need to be stiff but still light enough to go over the mountains; and in a three-week race, riders want to limit fatigue from harsh road vibrations. Most pro frames are made of aluminum, carbon fiber, or a combination of the two. Drawn hollow-aluminum tubes are shaped into complex cross sections that resist the torsional forces of pedaling. Carbon fiber frames are made by laying very thin sheets, or plies, of fiber in a mold and then applying high temperatures and pressure to set the resin adhesive. Carbon's advantage is that it can dampen vibration while remaining quite stiff. Frames today weigh as little as 2.1 pounds, complete bikes as little as 15 pounds.

Wheels: Physics tells us that rotating mass is more costly to a rider than static mass, so wheels must be light, but durable enough to stand up to rough roads. Carbon fiber is used here, as well, on the rim sections, which are sculpted into deep V shapes to slice the wind. Some wheels now use ceramic bearings, originally from aerospace applications, which can be made in tolerances 1,000 times smaller than steel. Some makers estimate that the decreased friction equals almost

Today's bikes are high-tech marvels, whether they're the American-made Trek, Specialized, and Cannondale machines or the classic Italian boutique rigs from De Rosa, Pinarello, and Colnago— all represented in the 2004 Tour. But, in the end, the only time the bike is more important than the rider is when the bike fails. The modern-day equivalent of the wheel flip that so frustrated Tullio Campagnolo is the quick bike change. When a rider has a problem, "a mechanical," as it's called, a team car with a roof rack full of spares pulls up alongside and a quick swap is made. (The

three-quarters of a pound in weight savings.

Gears: Modern bicycle drivetrains have twice as many gears as those old ten-speeds had. As in a Formula One car, shifting is accomplished from the handlebar; the brake levers feature inboard paddles that shift the gears easily without taking a hand off the bar, even under full power in a sprint at over 60 kph (40 mph). Team mechanics change gear sets as often as every day, depending on the terrain. Some rear cogs are made of light, strong titanium.

Tires: Even the humble tire is high tech. Kevlar beads protect against punctures better, and weigh less, than steel beads. The tread features as many as three different durometers, or densities, of rubber: hard in the center for decreased rolling resistance, and soft, sticky rubber on the shoulders for cornering ability. The twenty-one teams in the Tour will go through almost 800 tires during the race.

Pedals: Like ski boots and bindings, pedals and shoes work together for maximum power transfer. A cleat on the bottom of the shoe clicks into the pedal, so that riders have a stable platform and can pull up on the backside of the pedal stroke. Shoes feature ultra stiff carbon fiber soles.

There is one major difference between an F1 Ferrari and a Tour bike: Many of the bikes today's Tour stars ride are identical to those sold in high-end bike shops. Got $7,000? Good. You can ride the same rig as Lance Armstrong.

most common mechanical is a flat tire; other problems are generally the result of crashes.) A rider such as Lance Armstrong has an endless supply of custom-built bikes in the vehicle trailing just behind him, each one's saddle and handlebars perfectly adjusted. A lesser rider might be forced to swap for a more generic machine, and to make the proper adjustments on the fly. (Seat height can be altered as the rider pedals; one of the Tour's best balancing acts is when a mechanic hangs out the side of his car, making repairs at over 60 kph [40 mph] as the rider hangs on.) If Armstrong

Team directors spend as much time working out scenarios on their laptops— whether a rider is likely to succeed in a solo break- away, for example, based on his previous perfor- mance—as they do designing training rides and strategies.

should "mechanical" at a critical point and a spare bike isn't immediately available, he might take a bike from a teammate, who then drops back, retrieves Armstrong's spare, and pedals it up to the leader for another trade. (The unwritten rule that prohibits competing riders from taking advantage of crashes and bathroom breaks also applies to technical misfortune; when a top racer is swapping, the front of the pack will slow to allow him to catch up.) See chapter 7, page 125, for more on the etiquette of the Tour de France.

Do-It-Yourself Race Repairs

As with golfers and their clubs, riders have spe- cific bikes for specific tasks. A time trial bike is generally built to fit the rider in an aggressive, for- ward-leaning position. For hills, riders might have a special bike with extra-low gears. Race officials always face a delicate balancing act to ensure that no mechanical item gives a rider unfair advantage. In the old days, the task was easier: A rider had to finish not only on the bike he started with, but with everything he had been carrying at the beginning of the race. Riders were sometimes penalized even for having chucked a ruined and unusable tire.

Receiving assistance for repairs was also forbidden. This led to some astonishing feats of stubborn persistence. In 1913 Eugene Christophe—the French national champion, nick- named "Cri-Cri" by his fans—was leading the Tour in the Pyrenees. On the descent of the Tourmalet, his front fork cracked. The Frenchman shoul- dered his bike and walked eight miles to the nearest town, Sainte-Marie-de-Campan, where he found a blacksmith shop. With race officials watching him, Christophe undertook a four-hour repair. When one official attempted to leave for a quick sandwich, Christophe stared him down, exclaiming, "You've made me your prisoner—and now you're mine. You'll stay here and eat coal if you're hungry!" Once the repair was done, Christophe continued, but his lead—and chance of victory—was gone. Astonishingly, the same mechanical problem plagued the French rider again in 1919; again he made the repairs and again lost his opportunity to wear the yellow jersey. Christophe's reputation as the unluckiest man ever to ride the Tour de France was cemented in 1922, when he broke his fork again. This time, though, he gave up. Instead of making the repairs, he borrowed a bike from a village priest and pedaled it to the nearest town, where he formally withdrew.

Christophe's travails have made him a Tour immortal; the forge in Sainte-Marie-de-Campan is now a national monument and a key stop for two-wheeling pilgrims heading into the Pyrenees.

The newest technological frontiers in the Tour are off the bike. Riders are relying more and

Time trial bikes are aerodynamically designed to cheat the wind.

more on sophisticated electronics to communicate, strategize, and evaluate their performance. On-board computers now measure power output along with speed and distance. Nearly every Tour rider wears a heart rate monitor, which allows him to know exactly when (or if) he's reached his maximum yield. Team directors spend as much time working out scenarios on their laptops—whether a rider is likely to succeed in a solo breakaway, for example, based on his previous performance—as they do designing training rides and strategies.

The remarkable thing is how little all this has changed the essence of the Tour. Although today's Tour looks different from the ones Gino Bartali and Eugene Christophe rode, the transformations the race has undergone—both cultural and technological—mirror, but don't outpace, the changes in the world surrounding the Tour. Like the bikes themselves, the Tour has undergone many cosmetic and technological alterations, but what happens—the way the race unfolds—is fundamentally the same. The relationship between rider and fan, between the event and the society that cherishes it, has remained startlingly fixed. The Tour evolves just enough to keep pace with the times. The Tour constantly moves forward, but never faster than the men who ride it, or the world of which it is a part.

CHAPTER 5

How to Win in 12 Impossible Steps

"We have to ride like animals.
It's all part of the sport."
—HENRI PÉLISSIER, DURING THE 1925 TOUR

How do you win the Tour de France? Here are the short answers: Be tough. Be genetically blessed. Be ruthless. Be ready. Only the rider who possesses these four essential attributes—and in just the right quantities—will be able to take best advantage of the fifth necessity: luck. What these add up to is a day-to-day chess match, played out at violently high speeds.

Food on the fly
in a feed zone

Every time out, each team has to deploy its resources with nearly flawless precision, always playing to its own advantages. Until 2003 the strategy of Lance Armstrong and U.S. Postal was to combine the needed attributes to physically and strategically annihilate competitors. Armstrong would hold back in the initial flat stages, gauging the field. Then, on the hardest mountain days, protected by his Postal teammates, he would pedal ahead, outpacing even his strongest competitors. The message to his rivals was crystal clear: *You have no hope.* In 2001 a demoralized Jan Ullrich, having been outpaced by Armstrong throughout the race, graciously offered his hand to the Texan as they summitted Luz-Ardiden, in the Pyrenees, and from that point on, the rest of the peloton was competing for second place. Last year a less-than-perfect Armstrong was unable to muster his trademark mercilessness, but he compensated with an oversize helping of pure grit. It was enough to win, and—compared to his previous routs—more thrilling to see.

If a rider doesn't eat, he's likely to experience what cyclists call bonking.

Prep A Tour victory starts months before the first wheels spin out of *le départ* (the start line) in Paris. It begins not just with training, but with knowing how to train and what to train for. Although Greg LeMond deserves credit for being the first to narrow his focus exclusively to winning the Tour, Lance Armstrong has taken that idea to a higher level of refinement. Like his predecessors, LeMond prepared for the Tour by mainly racing early-season events. He'd generally skip the Giro d'Italia—going for the double isn't impossible, but entering the brutally difficult Italian race is not a great idea—and undertake either lesser multiday races or single-day contests known as the Classics. (The most famous and exciting of these is Paris-Roubaix, during

which riders pedal 275 kilometers over muddy cobblestones; keep it in mind, along with the Giro, for your second foray into bike racing fandom. The bloody event is nicknamed *l'Enfer du Nord*— The Hell of the North.) Lance Armstrong also races in the early season, but not to get himself into shape; for the most part *that* he's already done in training. Instead, he uses competition to test his own abilities in the heat of battle. A key event is the Dauphiné Libéré, a seven-day stage race, held a few weeks before the Tour, that includes some of the same climbs. Armstrong won it in 2002 and 2003; in 2004, Iban Mayo— a Spaniard who was expected to be one of the Texan's toughest competitors—took the event, only to falter in the Tour and drop out after stage 15.

Most of Armstrong's training is more specific and solitary, and other potential Tour winners are beginning to imitate it. Armstrong is known to ride more hours than, probably, any of his competitors in the off-season, tailoring those rides for specific needs: measuring fitness; building climbing ability; determining what's strong and what's not. It wouldn't be an exaggeration to say that every training ride Armstrong undertakes is a critical and conscious piece of the mosaic that makes up his Tour de France strategy.

Another thing Armstrong does to a greater degree than earlier Tour winners is scout the course. In *The Road to Paris,* a 2002 documentary that chronicled the Tour champ's training routine, a solitary Armstrong pedals up the Galibier in an April snowstorm. Team director Johan Bruyneel pulls up to his rider in a warm car.

"I want to go a little more," says the shivering Armstrong.

"Why don't you do another ten kilometers of uphills?" Bruyneel suggests.

"I'll go down ten and come back," Armstrong replies, then turns around and vanishes in the fog. Bruyneel turns to the camera. "That," he says, "is what it takes to win the Tour de France."

A springtime scouting expedition pays off in July. Having ridden the climbs can give a rider an advantage over a racer who has only looked at the course profiles and anticipated the climb in conversation. It helps to be aware, for example, that an ascent categorized as a relatively easy portion of a fundamentally flat day, actually has a single, short, but brutally steep section, making it a perfect spot for a little intimidating acceleration. Anyone who hopes to win the Tour needs a detailed, leave-no-stone-unturned master plan. Armstrong learned this the hard way: In his first attempt at the French classic, in 1993, he became the youngest rider ever to win a stage—an impressive accomplishment—but had to withdraw a few days later, exhausted from going all out all the time. (Another stage winner that year was Bruyneel, who finished seventh overall.) The Tour de France does not forgive even a single, misbegotten episode of adrenaline-driven machismo.

A rider in contention is constantly thinking: What's the payoff if I attack? What's the cost? Every move must result in a net competitive gain. For instance, Jan Ullrich's 2003 strategy was based on a mental game. He never claimed he had a chance to win, saying that a top-twenty finish would be satisfactory. It wasn't that the other race leaders didn't notice the German hovering at the front of the pack. Nor did they dare underestimate him. But his deception worked to shift the focus to moves being made by other contenders. This gave the 1997 Tour winner the chance to implement the rest of his plan. Knowing that, at best, he'd be able to match Armstrong in the hills, Ullrich pounced in the first time trial, putting the yellow jersey into serious play for the first time in five years. That Ullrich ultimately lost doesn't signal a defect in his tactics: He fulfilled his initial desire to finish well, and he put the world on notice for 2004. But Ullrich wasn't able to keep a low profile after that, and the Texan proceeded to hammer him, hard, in the early stages. The anticipated shootout at high noon clearly went to the cowboy.

Everyday Rituals

What's the most important off-bike aspect of the Tour? Food. What can put a contender out of the race with just a single mistake? Food. Nobody can win the Tour without eating properly and eating carefully. Even the flattest Tour stages burn up more than 6,000 calories—about triple what the average American takes in each day. A hard day in the mountains can require over 10,000 calories. The body can store, at most, about 1,500 calories. You do the math. Because of the size of the human "gas tank,"

Racer Robert Jacquinot on a soup break in the early 1920s

racers have to constantly work to keep it topped off. If a rider doesn't eat, he's likely to experience what cyclists call bonking. That's when the body runs completely out of carbs. Besides diminishing the ability to mount muscular effort, the bonk also affects brain function: Thinking becomes difficult and the rider feels as though he's in a haze. This can seriously jeopardize his ability to finish the stage, let alone the entire race. In 2000 Armstrong famously bonked on the final climb of a stage and was, for one rare occasion, in jeopardy of losing his overall race lead. A rider who's been eating properly should *never* bonk while competing, but it does happen. When it does, the only thing to do is eat and try to keep moving forward for the fifteen or twenty minutes it takes to recover. (Bonking is a funny thing: When it happens, you feel paralyzed; all you want is to lie down by the side of the road and die. But eat a few cookies and pretty soon you'll be wondering what the problem was.)

During the race, riders get most of their nutrition from sports drinks. Armstrong often uses the basic stuff you can buy in your local convenience store, although each rider has specific preferences, ranging from high-tech powdered mixes to rather off-putting blends of soft drinks or juices. One of the most effective drinking strategies is to mix a beverage that's about 80 percent carb and 20 percent protein, since a little bit of the latter markedly speeds absorption of the former.

For solid foods, the current trend is toward easily digested energy gels (we're using the term "solid" very loosely here; the substance is more like a slimy pudding). These are almost pure glucose, plus vitamins and minerals. Some also include caffeine, a restricted substance of which the riders are allowed to consume no more than the equivalent of a few cups of coffee daily. The composition of the gels makes them a milder, legal

version of the caffeine-laced, nitroglycerin-coated sugar cubes used by earlier tour racers—sometimes washed down with their preferred sports drink, Vin Mariani, an energizing blend of wine and coca leaves. The use of high-tech sports foods is relatively new to the Tour, though. Even today, some riders still consume the more traditional Tour diet: rice cakes with jam, small sandwiches, and fruit. Eating is a personalized routine, and riders need to go with what makes them feel the best. The middle of the Tour de France is no time to start toying with your digestive functions.

Eating during the race is a ritualized procedure. Every Tour stage has at least one feed zone, usually in a low-key part of the route, where team officials wait for the riders to pass, and hand them *musettes*—canvas or nylon sacks—filled with snacks. At other times a *domestique* will pedal up from the team car with a slew of lunchbags slung over his shoulder and water bottles stuffed into his jersey pockets. (Another term for *domestique* is "water carrier.")

A domestique carries *musettes* filled with food and water to his teammates at the head of the pack.

Mario Cipollini and mates winning a 1993 team time trial

Once the race has ended, the team members return to their hotels (which can be surprisingly low-budget), where each rider turns his uniform in for washing, or, on less well-heeled teams, rinses it himself. Next comes a massage from the team *soigneur,* who's sort of an old-school body-work expert. The rubdown is very sport-specific, concentrating on flexing, stretching, and revitalizing the legs. Riders who are scraped up (the proper term is "road rash") are rebandaged. One Tour subplot is the ever-increasing count of riders with scabbed arms and legs wrapped in gauze and nylon netting.

Just before bedtime, the team eats together. It would be unusual to see riders popping into a local restaurant for dinner even if they had the energy. In the old days, dining out was a high-risk proposition, since local saboteurs often poisoned the food. (Even now there remains a taboo against accepting water bottles from fans, who nevertheless continue to offer them.) Instead, a team will eat a classic cyclist's high-carb supper: lots of rice, pasta, and potatoes, with some chicken or eggs on the side. Breakfast is similar, although cereal is usually added.

Finally, there's sleep—or the attempt to sleep. The Tour is just too hard, too unnerving, and too stressful to allow proper rest. Forget about sleep aids, whether they're prescription, over the counter, or herbal; no rider would risk a possible positive drug test by using them. But you have to try to sleep, even though your mind is racing faster than you ever were, filled with images of screaming fans and high-speed descents where you almost wiped out. Even the mere act of lying in bed is difficult, because you're so sunburned and saddle sore. What do you do? You do your best, and take comfort in knowing that every other racer is undergoing the same nocturnal torture.

Controlling the Variables

Obviously, controlling these variables is critical because doing so maximizes the good breaks that come a rider's way and can neutralize the bad ones. For instance, in 1979 Bernard Hinault lost the yellow jersey after some bad luck (a flat tire) but chased his rival, Joop Zoetemelk, until the stage-15 mountain time trial, a 55-kilometer uphill test. Hinault rode calmly and smoothly and dismantled his Dutch rival, gaining more than two minutes and proceeding to win the Tour. Hinault knew exactly what he was capable of, and was confident that he'd prepared for the moment when he needed to win. (Hinault's ability to grind down his rivals, slowly and methodically, and the perpetual scowl he wore when riding, earned him his nickname, "The Badger.")

Another example of strategic savvy occurred in 1996, when Miguel Indurain (the last rider

Hail to the Loser!

In a culture like America's, where second place just isn't good enough and tying is like kissing your sister, the idea of celebrating the last-place finisher might seem perverse. In the Tour de France, however, the battle to finish in last place for the entire race—to be *la lanterne rouge*, the light on the caboose—is a heroic subplot of its own.

Over time, the *lanterne rouge* has come to signify the idea that merely to reach the finish in Paris, even hours behind the winner, is a huge accomplishment. "I have this title now and I'm not giving it to someone else," said Hans De Clercq, the winner of 2003's title. Speaking late in the race to the Belgian sports newspaper *Het Laatste Nieuws*, he outlined the philosophy and strategy—with a wink. "Nobody dreams of being the very last rider in the Tour, but once you're there you come to like it. Conquering the title is easy; keeping it is much more

difficult: The ideal Lanterne has to finish every day on time, but not earlier than strictly necessary." Many riders will tell you that, if given the grim choice, finishing the Tour in last place would be better than winning a stage but later quitting the race.

Riders must finish each day's stage within a percentage of the stage-winner's time (the actual number varies based on length and difficulty of the stage). Those who don't are disqualified. In the mountains, this is exceedingly difficult, and the *lanterne* must lose as much time as possible without going over the limit. A large digital clock sits over the finish line of each stage, ticking off time until the limit is reached, at which point it goes blank. To riders approaching the finish, only to see the clock "rolled over black," the disappointment is huge. They can go home.

The nonclimbers must be mathematicians, calculating how fast they must ride to avoid elimination,

before Armstrong to win five Tours) faltered in the mountains. Bjarne Riis—who, at the age of thirty-two, was not considered a major threat to win the Tour—seized the opportunity. On a day when a long stage, more than 160 kilometers, was abbreviated to just 45 kilometers because the Alpine passes on the route were snowed under, Riis, blessed with a powerful sprint, extended his lead and ultimately became the first and only Dane to win the Tour.

yet not struggle so hard that they fatigue themselves too much for the next day's stage. Canadian Alex Stieda, who on the first stage of the 1986 Tour became the first North American rider to wear the yellow jersey, said that the Dutch rider Gerrie Kneteman, a talented sprinter who had won 10 stages of the Tour and worn yellow three times, told him that to prove himself worthy of the leader's jersey, he had to finish the race.

"When we entered the Pyrenees, Gerrie told me how to pace myself during a Tour de France mountain stage," recalled Stieda. "I was told that we would lose five minutes on the first climb, gain back three minutes on the descent and flats to the next climb, lose eight minutes on the next, more difficult climb, gain back five, and that would leave fifteen minutes to finish within the time limit! All very calm and calculated. He knew that I wasn't a climber; we were both 'utilitarian' riders who just

needed to survive the mountains and finish within each day's time limit so that we could help our team on the flats and rolling stages later on." Stieda, whose 1986 Tour was his first and only participation, missed becoming the *lanterne rouge*, rolling into Paris in 120th place.

In the last couple of days of the race, when the pace has relaxed and people have a good sense of where they're going to finish, the battle for last place can produce some amusing jockeying for position. In 2002 Latvia's Arvis Piziks and Spain's Igor Flores played out a hilarious battle for the *lanterne*. On the Tour's final day, Piziks, pedaling into the wind in the penultimate position, tired and sat up on his bike, instantly slowing down. Flores assumed that Piziks was slowing in order to sneak below him, so the Spaniard slowed, too. The two dueled it out, slower and slower, almost coming to a stop, until Piziks, grinning, gave it up and let Flores "pass"—behind him.

Of course, bad luck happens, too. Pedro Delgado won the 1988 Tour, but tarnished his victory when a blood test revealed a small quantity of probenicid, an agent that masks steroid use. The drug was so new that it hadn't yet been officially banned, and Delgado was allowed to continue. (Delgado's case is a good example of the cat-and-mouse game sometimes played between athletes and officials; if a drug is easy to detect, another drug that hides the first drug may be used—at least until the race *commissaires* come up with a test for the drug that's designed to foil the other test.) The next year, in what could only be called a further self-sabotaging Freudian slip, Delgado, having vowed to prove that his earlier victory was legitimate, was doing a television interview when his start time for the prologue came. Delgado stayed in the race, to finish third, but by effectively taking himself out of the running, he left the field open for another rider to take advantage: That was Greg LeMond, who edged Laurent Fignon in the now famous time trial into Paris.

Riders, Races, and Reasons

Riders have goals other than winning the Tour. The prize could be a stage win on what are usually, but not always, futile breakaways. Over and over again, on the flats, you'll see comparatively obscure riders sailing forward, sometimes alone, sometimes with others. (Watch closely, though, because nearly every year somebody does the impossible

Grit, grit, and more grit.

and manages to keep the pack at bay all the way to the finish line.) If you're going for the green sprint jersey (decided by measuring which riders are fastest in reaching a series of predetermined sprinting sections of the course) or the climber's jersey, you'll use an entirely different set of tactics than somebody who's competing for the stage win or the *maillot jaune*. In effect, you're competing in different races.

Sprint wins are among the Tour's most exciting and dangerous. Dozens of riders jockey for position, trying to avoid being in front—where the wind resistance is greatest—and measuring their rivals, waiting for the right moment. Then there's an explosive acceleration, and the riders make for the finish line in an all-out attack. If one rider goes down in a sprint, nearly everyone behind him will follow. A single sprint crash can injure or take out a dozen or more riders. Tyler Hamilton's broken collarbone in 2003 came during one of those breakneck finishes. One of the greatest sprinters of all time is Mario Cipollini, who leads all active Tour de France sprinters with 12 stage victories, although he didn't participate in 2003 and likely won't appear in 2004. (He and Tour director Jean-Marie Leblanc have an ongoing conflict, because "Cipo" nearly always quits the race in the mountains. Like Desgrange, today's Tour chieftain has little respect for those who don't grit out the entire race.) Another specialist is Frenchman Richard Virenque. He's never won the Tour, but he's taken six polka dot jerseys—and the attempts to win them are some of the most excruciating, strategic battles of the Tour.

For some riders, the object is merely to survive. "Mere" survival is itself a lofty ambition.

Mario Cipollini, best active Tour sprinter and thorn-in-the-side of race officials

Young riders, who typically pedal too hard too early, who can't modulate their aggressive instincts, aren't a good bet to complete. They go hard, and the mountains annihilate them. Quitting the tour (as many as a quarter of the riders do it every year) is a public act. A van called *la voiture balai*, or broom wagon, "sweeps up" the rear of the course, collecting racers who have reached their limit. As if dropping out isn't ignominious in and of itself, a television crew is usually there to record the humiliation. (The feature-length animated French movie *The Triplets of Belleville* exploits the ritual with perverse pathos.) Only the most elite riders are spared; they're allowed to slip, hopefully without anyone watching, into a team car.

For those who survive, finishing is more than a case of having limped into Paris after everyone else went home. Every rider who reaches the Champs-Élysées has managed to stay under the official time limit—meaning he's ridden fast enough to not be eliminated, usually reaching the finish line no more than 10 percent slower than the day's leader—and he'll forever be known as someone who completed one of the most torturous rituals humankind ever invented.

CHAPTER 6

Climb and Punishment

"In the history of human affairs, does not the ascent of the Galibier on bicycles constitute the first triumph of mortal intelligence over the laws of gravity?"

—Henri Desgrange, 1911

Welcome to the "Circle of Death." Ever since the Tour de France first tackled the Pyrenees and the Alps, this has been the salutation for the race's most magnificent stages. The mountain stages combine excitement and fear, teamwork and solitary labor, pain and exultation. They're where the Tour de France story reaches literal and narrative heights. Take Greg LeMond's 1991 blowup: LeMond attacked

Crossing the Tourmalet pass in 1924

brilliantly on the Tourmalet, looking every bit the dominant champion, yet, one peak later, drained, he self-destructed. The Circle of Death had claimed another victim, and the first American to win the Tour de France would never again contend in the race.

Better yet, take the drama that came to pass in the Alps twelve years later, during the centenary Tour de France. In the second week of a race that roughly followed the 1903 route of the first Tour de France, crashes, mad sprints, and grueling climbs all played out on winding roads lined by nearly 1 million spectators. In some spots, viewers assembled so thickly it was as if a wall of bodies and noise lined the course. The Tour de France was about to unleash its most furious weapon on its participants. Indeed, this last day in the towering Alps would turn out to be terribly, tragically cruel. It would be as if everything that had ever been possible in 100 years of bike racing had somehow been encapsulated and molded into a single, emotion-filled afternoon. When it ended, nobody—not riders, not race officials, or the crowd—could believe it.

The race began with two massive climbs. Both the Col du Lauteret and the Col d'Izoard are legendary ascents, jagged upthrusts with grades that sometimes exceed 10 percent. The Col d'Izoard, especially, is steeped in Tour tradition. The top of the hill is called the *Sommet des Anges*, Summit of the Angels, after Luxembourg rider Charly Gaul, winner of the 1958 Tour de France. Climbing through freezing rain, Gaul maintained an impossibly calm demeanor and silky pedaling style. "It was," an observer remarked, commenting on Gaul's victory, "as if he were an angel himself."

Lance Armstrong knew how to dominate the climbs that way. He'd won the previous four tours by pedaling away from his rivals in the Alps,

One of the unique attributes of a bike race is fluidity. One mountain earlier, Beloki had been part of the group trying to demoralize Armstrong. Now the two needed each other.

mounting aggressive, demoralizing attacks—pushes forward, away from the group—that even his most formidable competitors couldn't match. It was what Armstrong had been expected to do in 2003, but now, after three days in the mountains, it hadn't happened. Instead it was Armstrong's rivals who were attacking, testing the Texan, over and over, on the 180-kilometer stage. Armstrong matched each assault. Despite brutal heat—it was nearly 100 degrees—the attacks continued up the first two Cols, as the riders gained more than 3,000 meters of elevation.

With so thin a lead, Armstrong seemed vulnerable for the first time. Racers who might otherwise have settled for second began contemplating their chances of beating the champion to Paris, of denying his attempt to match the record for the most-ever Tour de France wins. Primary among those who began to believe Armstrong was beatable was a tiny Spaniard named Joseba Beloki, who had finished second the previous year. Throughout the day, Beloki attacked, gaining on

The peloton pushes up the Pyrenees.

The pack climbs Puerto de la Bonaigua pass in Spain in 1993.

Armstrong. His thrusts were matched by similar pushes from Kazak rider Alexandre Vinokourov and American Tyler Hamilton, who was racing with a broken collarbone (that he was even in the race, let alone among the leaders, was astonishing). Was Armstrong wilting in the heat? Hiding an injury? Playing possum? Speculation blossomed.

In the altitude profiles each fan carried—during the Tour, some French newspapers turned as much as 90 percent of their editorial space over to the race, publishing detailed maps, timing charts, and thousands of lines of prognostication and punditry—the day's final climb was portrayed as mild. The Côte de la Rochette rose less than 400 meters. But after 160 kilometers of pedaling at speeds that sometimes exceeded 48 kph (30 mph), even a relatively small hill would be torture. Following the ascent, the riders would at least have a fast downhill to the finish line in the town of Gap.

As the riders neared the finish, Vinokourov sprinted away from the field, believing he had enough energy to outrun any riders who wanted to chase him up and over the hill. Several followed, but by the time the climbing began, Armstrong and Beloki had outrun the main pursuit group by 15 seconds. They were one-half minute behind Vinokourov. One of the unique attributes of a bike race is fluidity. One mountain earlier, Beloki had been part of the group trying to demoralize Armstrong. Now the two needed each other. Switching places as they pedaled (a following rider uses as much as 30 percent less energy because of improved aerodynamics), the Spaniard and the American formed an alliance. The two crested la Rochette together.

The descent was picture-perfect Tour de France: high speed and physical intensity against a pastoral backdrop. Curving downward, the two riders reached speeds of 65 kph (40 mph). If you observe the Tour carefully, you might come to believe that every road in France is glassy smooth, without a pothole or rut. In fact, the Tour is so important that nearly any road it travels (except for ones intentionally made difficult, like those with cobblestones, for instance) has to be perfect; rural lanes, such as the one descending into Gap, are often resurfaced just before the race. Today, though, the blazing sun was turning the freshly laid tar into sticky patches. There was no other way to put it—the road was melting.

Hamilton and Armstrong pursue Beloki in 2003 before Beloki's crash.

Armstrong and Beloki approached a switchback. The Spaniard was leading Armstrong by two bike lengths, and Vinokourov, still in front, had just disappeared behind the curve. Suddenly the glistening tar caught Beloki's tire and his back wheel fishtailed. Beloki swung left, nearly righted himself, then, like a pendulum, swung in the opposite direction. His bike was nearly perpendicular to the route. The intense friction of his braking had turned him at an angle—and his tire rolled off the rim.

Controlling a bike in such conditions is almost impossible. Beloki hit the ground hard. Armstrong—nearly on top of his rival—swerved left; there was no place to go but off the road, and he torpedoed into a plowed field. Riding on both instinct and skill (he had raced cyclocross, a specialized event that involves dirt surfaces and frequent dismounts to carry bikes over obstacles), Armstrong pointed down the bumpy slope toward the opposite side of the switchback, leaped off his bike and over a small ditch, smoothly remounted his machine, and emerged on the road in the thick of the chase group, which had caught up to the scene. The Tour de France had never seen such an astonishing example of bike handling. The crowd was both stunned and thrilled.

That excitement turned quickly to heartbreak. Even television viewers could hear Beloki's agonized cries. He'd broken his femur, wrist, collarbone, and elbow. And he'd lost his chance— a great chance. Beloki's teammates gathered around him, even though by stopping they, too were risking elimination. It was as if the race had suddenly vaporized; spectators, race officials, and teammates were in tears. Armstrong continued with the rest of the pack, but as the riders were informed of Beloki's injuries via the tiny radios they carry, sadness dulled the approach

. . . the Circle of Death isn't about separating the men from the boys, but rather the winners from the men.

to Gap. Vinokourov finished 36 seconds ahead of Armstrong. The Texan still led the race, but by a margin so slim that even a single mechanical problem could throw the event to a new victor. He'd never emerged from the mountains so vulnerable.

Beloki could no longer take advantage of that. Instead, Vinokourov—who would eventually finish third—emerged as a new threat. Tour de France aficionados view such changes of fortune with an existential shrug—*C'est la Tour*—but nobody who heard Beloki's cries could help but feel that on this day fate had dealt out an extra measure of malice. Most also agreed it was one of the most exciting days in Tour de France history. But with nearly two weeks until the Paris finale, there was much more to come.

Kings of the Hill

Why are the mountains so important? Use your own bike-riding experiences as a guide. Remember that massive hill in your neighborhood, the one you'd pedal a mile out of your way to climb? Remember how much your legs burned, how good you felt when you finally reached the top?

That childhood experience lives deep in the soul of every Tour de France climb. But no one's kidding around; the Circle of Death isn't about separating the men from the boys, but rather the winners from the men. The big climbs come on days when the competitors have already pedaled 160 kilometers or more. They're at the brink of exhaustion and now they have to pedal, and fast. There's almost no way to express in words—and you can't detect it on television—how quickly Lance Armstrong, Tyler Hamilton, and specialists such as Colombian Roberto Heras or France's Richard Virenque (the Tour's most legendary climber of recent years) move up these hills. First

Five Legendary Climbs

The mountain passes have been a part of the Tour since 1906, when the race first ventured to higher ground on the Ballon d'Alsace. These are five of the most famous climbs.

Col du Telegraphe/Col du Galibier: 28.5 kilometers, average grade 6.8 percent

When approached from the Telegraphe side, these two climbs combine to form a monster: 28.5 kilometers of climbing with grades as steep as 10 percent. When first ridden (it is one of the older climbs in the Tour), it was still a dirt road. At the top of the Galibier is a monument to Tour founder Henri Desgrange. The Galibier does not now figure in many Tour finishes, but it was here, in 1957, that Jacques Anquetil established his dominance, en route to the first of his five Tour wins.

Col du Galibier

Col du Tourmalet: 15 kilometers, average grade 5.7 percent

The Tourmalet was one of the first Pyrenean mountains included, in the 1910 Tour. The French press thought the route so difficult that it dubbed the stage the "Circle of Death." It's also where, in 1913, Eugene Christophe broke his fork and reforged it in the village of Sainte-Marie-de-Campan. The Tourmalet also goes by the name La Mongie, which is the ski area near the top. In 1969 Eddy Merckx crushed his rivals here as part of a 145-kilometer attack. But perhaps the best story is from that 1910 Tour, when Octave Lapize, who would later go on to win the Tour, ground his bike past race officials and spat "Assassins!" at them.

Col d'Izoard: 19.3 kilometers, average grade 5.9 percent

One of the fiercest and steepest of the Alpine climbs, the Izoard has changed the face of many a Tour. Three-time champion Louison Bobet was famous for launching his race-winning attacks on the Izoard, and one of the key battles of 1989 played out here between Greg LeMond and Laurent Fignon. LeMond attacked hard on the Izoard and gained time, only to lose it the next day on the Alpe d'Huez. And in 1975 Bernard Thévenet attacked Eddy Merckx here as Merckx was gunning for his sixth Tour win. Merckx lost the lead that day and never regained it.

Mont Ventoux: 21 kilometers, average grade 7.5 percent

Mont Ventoux, the hulking giant of Provence, named for the winds that sweep its treeless summit, didn't appear in the 2003 or 2004 climbs, and isn't scheduled for 2005. This volcanic oddity rises from the sunflower fields that so fascinated the impressionist painters. The impression Ventoux leaves is of pain. Though the mountain isn't as high as the Alps, its limestone-scattered upper reaches turn it into a bleached, roasting, oxygen-deprived moonscape. Unlike other mountain stages, which feature several large climbs, Ventoux stands alone at the end of a long, flatter stage—but that doesn't make it less hard.

In 1967, it was in the heat of Ventoux that Tom Simpson, who five years earlier had become the first Englishman to wear the yellow jersey, attempted to catch Raymond Poulidor's breakaway. The perennial Tour runner-up was powering toward the mountain's 1,890-meter summit, and Simpson was trying with all his might to reel his rival in. A few kilometers from the top, the British rider collapsed. "Put me back on my bike," he pleaded. He pedaled another kilometer, then crumbled. Efforts to resuscitate him failed (amphetamines were later implicated in his death) and Simpson became the first Tour fatality in forty years. A stone memorial near the final switchback marks the spot where Simpson fell.

The Tour's southernmost climb has vexed Lance Armstrong. He has never won there, and he's been frustrated by that. Since Ventoux isn't in this year's event, Armstrong has to be wondering if he'll ever add a triumph on this legendary ascent to his Tour accomplishments.

Alpe d'Huez: 13.8 kilometers, average grade 7.9 percent

The Alpe, not used till the 1952 Tour, is the most storied of climbs. Others are steeper and longer, but none occupies such a place in the hearts and minds of Tour fans. The Alpe was the first mountaintop finish in the Tour, and as such it is one of the most exciting. Built onto a steep hillside leading to a ski resort, the road features the famous twenty-one switchbacks. The first winner here was none other than the great Fausto Coppi. In the years since, it has changed the face of every edition that passes over it. Greg LeMond almost lost the 1986 and 1989 Tours here, and in 2001 Lance Armstrong pulled his famous bluff, feigning poor form before attacking Jan Ullrich early on the climb and soloing to victory.

you become aware of their discouraging presence over your shoulder. Next thing you know, they're not only passing you, but—it dawns grimly on you—they're going *twice as fast as you are*. The best climbers move so quickly up the hills that their speeds stun spectators along the route; you can see their incredulous faces.

Climbers in the Tour de France fall into a couple of categories. Some are contenders for the yellow jersey. Others are all about the hills, and only the hills, as they compete for the polka dot King of the Mountains (KOM) jersey—the *maillot à pois*—or a glorious stage win on one of the legendary summits. (By the way, the oddly psychedelic *maillot à pois* hasn't always been associated with the climbing competition, which dates back to 1933. Polka dots entered the picture in 1975 after a candy company took over sponsorship of the prize and introduced a design resembling its packaging.) For a yellow jersey contender, the key aim is not to crack. Fail in the mountains and you're likely to lose so much time that you'll never recover. The way to prevent this is *not* to be the best climber in the race. That's for the specialists, who are likely to be too small—not powerful enough in the sprints and time trials—to win the general classification. The proper strategy is to use your teammates, the top-notch mountain goats on your squad, to shuttle you upward. They'll ride just in front of you, taking turns "pulling" you higher, while you save energy. You'll need it to answer breakaways en route, and especially as the *arrivée* nears, when your helpers slip away, exhausted, and the best riders in the pack hurtle toward the finish line, looking to gain precious seconds.

The best way to illustrate the challenge is to introduce its physical embodiment, Richard Virenque, the French rider who has won the King

of the Mountains jersey seven times, something
no other rider has done. Virenque, who retired
after the 2004 race, had gotten so good at taking
the climbing prize that his victory in the mountains had become as expected as the yellow
jersey is for Lance Armstrong. The French were
grateful for this preeminence, since the Tour's
host country has been going through a *maillot
jaune* drought for almost two decades. Thomas
Voeckler's stellar performance early in the 2004
Tour sated some of that desire for the yellow,
but Virenque's career finale provided the most
sentimental excitement.

When Virenque is climbing well, it's an inspir-
ing sight. His ascent during the 2003 Tour's 7th
stage was a classic vision of the climber's fluidity,
a good example of why the best mountain riders
are nicknamed "angels." Virenque's smooth and
seemingly (only seemingly!) effortless pedaling
style, or "spin," carried him up the hill toward an

**Another
victory** in the
bank for Virenque

uncontested stage win and
a 24-hour sojourn in yellow.
Virenque paid handsomely
the next day when he nearly
cracked as the race continued
through the Alps, but his careful strategizing earned him the
right to wear "his" jersey in
Paris again. (Remember, the
KOM prize is awarded by a
points system that scores the
full range of Tour ascents, not
only the ones in the major
mountain ranges.) Virenque's
assault on the mountains was
utterly devastating to his
rivals: The Frenchman col-
lected 324 climbing points; no
other competitor reached 200.

Fail in the mountains and you're likely to lose so much time that you'll never recover. The way to prevent this is not to be the best climber in the race.

Know the Score

Scoring the KOM is a bit arcane, but it's fairly simple once you understand the thinking behind it. Most climbs with more than 90 meters (300 ft) of elevation gain are rated. Climbs up to 300 meters (1,000 vertical feet) are assigned to the fourth (easiest) category. Categories three through one indicate minimum altitudes of about 600, 1,000, and 1,500 meters (2,000, 3,500, and 5,000 ft). Higher than that and the climb is "beyond category": *hors categorie* or "HC," as you'll see it marked on Tour de France route maps. These are just guidelines. There's a certain amount of art involved in determining a climb's category, and the same hill can be categorized differently from year to year, depending on when the climb appears during the race (a smaller ascent at the end of a long day might be rated tougher than a bigger one early on) and the condition of the road.

Following a favorite rider is a worthwhile sideshow to the Tour's main event, and evidence of dramatic and beloved rides can literally be seen on the road. Chalking a favorite racer's name on the pavement is a long-standing Tour custom. Lance Armstrong recalls being inspired by seeing the faint remnants of his name, from previous races, as he worked to recover his fitness after beating cancer.

The outpouring of love directed at Virenque as he raced the last Tour de France of his career was a perfect example of the race's emotional complexity. The Frenchman sullied his name in 1998, when he was thrown out of the Tour, along with the rest of his team, for taking illegal drugs; he proclaimed his innocence louder and longer than any of his compatriots, then finally confessed.

The fiasco meant Virenque had plenty to prove when he returned to competition, and prove it he did. By 2002, when he edged Lance Armstrong in an infernolike march up Mont Ventoux, all was forgiven. The French had their Tour hero. No matter that he was a specialist;

Light reading
to thank—and encourage—the competitors

his pain and suffering, both physical and emotional, were the stuff Tour legends are made of. Virenque's comeback is something several of today's riders—including the Briton David Millar, whose friendly, hip demeanor and sprinting power made him an up-and-coming favorite until he admitted drug use and was banned for the 2005 and 2006 seasons—are hoping to emulate as they emerge from exile.

The Majesty and the Masochism
What is it like to climb a Tour de France peak? Be glad you'll probably never know. But come with me, anyway, for a virtual ascent as we pedal up Alpe d'Huez. We'll start our day's ride at the bottom of the famous mountain, then pedal to the end of the road, to a ski village that is generally rather sedate during the summertime, except for one day. As we depart the tiny village of Bourg d'Oisans, we pedal terrain that slopes gently upward. Farmhouses and cultivated fields soon give way to sparkling green woodland. But the low-key ascension soon ends, and we're faced with what might be cycling's most demoralizing vista: twenty-one switchbacks, as neatly stacked as slices of bread, rising more than 2,000 feet above us. I comfort you by mentioning that the climb isn't terribly long, as these things go—only about 9 miles—but with the grade averaging 8 percent, you'll soon discover the

Lance, in yellow, leads Jan Ullrich uphill in 2003.

absolute limits of your endurance. You'll get only a few hundred yards before you're begging for mercy. Don't feel bad—it's hell even for those of us who do it for a living. If you persevere, you'll find yourself, as you slowly mount, wondering how time itself slowed down. And how distances grew. The next switchback isn't far—you could throw a baseball to it—so why isn't it getting any closer? Each turn is an exercise in balance; you're leaning, as you curve around, but at least you can move a bit faster. You don't get a chance to enjoy it, though—the straight-ahead climbing has begun again. And again. Again. One more thing: Try not to worry about the wind, which is likely to gust harder the higher you get. Your consolation as a recreational rider? A photographer is stationed on the second-to-last switchback before the summit. He'll snap a picture of you looking worse than you thought possible, and after you've recovered in town with a beer and a plate of spaghetti, you can head over to the photo shop, plunk down 10 Euros or so, and have a permanent memento of your ordeal.

Whether you're a Tour de France racer or a recreational rider, the only way to pedal to the top of any mountain is to ride *your* ride. Pedal at the pace that works for you, and don't let ego or pride whip you into a foolish and futile expenditure of energy. The fastest way to crack on a Tour de France climb is to try to maintain somebody else's tempo. It's hard enough to stick to your own.

Does it hurt? Don't ask. And don't think for a moment that the pros aren't suffering mightily. What distinguishes you from the racers is not their ability to climb without agony—it's their ability to endure the agony. But there's more. To win in the mountains, merely tolerating the pain isn't nearly enough. You have to live for it. You have to love it.

The great Alpine peaks all possess their own uniquely sadistic qualities. The 2005 riders submit to the one-two punch of the Col du Télégraphe and the Col du Galibier. The Télégraphe slope is comparatively short, covering 12 kilometers at a 6.7 percent grade. There's a brief reprieve for the riders as they descend the summit, and then comes the monster: Galibier's average grade of 6.9 percent isn't much more than Télégraphe's, but it is longer—17 kilometers—and has several wall-like sections where the pitch exceeds 10 percent.

What to Watch for in 2005

Two of the tour's most legendary climbs didn't make the 2005 agenda. Alpe d'Huez, site of last

Lance Armstrong, Marco Pantani, and Richard Virenque climb the Combespinasse together during the 14th stage of 1994's Tour de France.

Author Bob Roll vanquishing Col de la Colombière in 1990

year's chaotic time trial, is off the list, and once again Mont Ventoux—an overheated ascent in Provence that has frequently vexed Armstrong— has also been excluded. But the 2005 Tour brings back one of the event's most forbidding and unfor- giving ascents, the Col du Galibier. Whether you're riding from the north or south, the Col du Galibier is pure evil, miles of exposed switchbacks inter- spersed between agonizingly steep straight stretches. The views are amazing, with glaciers and snowy vistas all around, but Tour riders rarely get to appreciate them. Even if the pavement weren't lined with spectators blocking the view, the suffering is so great that it is nearly blinding. The mountains demand complete attention on the downhill, as well. The best descenders—those with mountain bike or ski experience often excel—can make up considerable time over their more tenta- tive rivals, but the cost of a mistake is huge when top speeds of 97 kph (60 mph) are reached by com- petitors wearing nothing but thin Lycra and helmets basically made of brightly colored Styrofoam.

The 2005 Tour, as in 2004, is designed to intensify the pain usually inflicted by the mountains. The riders enter the Alps, and then almost immediately visit the Pyrenees. On Wednesday, July 13, stage 11, the riders tackle one of the Tour's classic trios: the brutal combination of the

Wait Till the Year

One climb that hasn't appeared in recent Tours, and isn't scheduled for 2005, is Mt. Ventoux, the hulking giant of Provence. This peak rises in isolation from the sunflower fields that so fascinated the impressionist painters. The impression Ventoux leaves is of nothing but pain. Though the mountain isn't as high as the Alps, its limestone-scattered upper reaches turn it into a bleached, roasting moonscape. In 1967, it was in the heat of Ventoux that Tom Simpson, who five years earlier had become the first Englishman to wear the yellow jersey, attempted to catch Raymond Poulidor's breakaway. The perennial Tour runner-up was powering toward the mountain's 1,890-meter summit, and Simpson was trying with all his might to reel his rival in. A few kilometers from the top, the British rider collapsed. "Put me back on my bike," he pleaded. He pedaled another kilometer, then crumbled. Efforts to resuscitate him failed (amphetamines were later implicated in his death) and Simpson became the first Tour fatality in forty years. A stone memorial near the final switchback marks the spot where Simpson fell.

The Tour's southernmost climb has vexed Lance Armstrong. He has never won there, and he's been frustrated by that. Since Ventoux isn't in this year's event, it now seems likely that Armstrong might never get something he's always said he wants—a decisive win on the Provençal summit.

Col de la Madeleine, the Col du Télégraphe, and the Col du Galibier. The first two climbs are hard enough, ascending more than 3,500 meters over nearly 65 kilometers. But as the riders leave the ski resort of Valoire, they'll be pedaling the brutal Galibier, a monster with switchbacks over and over along 17.5 steep kilometers, for a total altitude gain of 2,645 meters. It will likely be a hot day, and the afternoon sun will quickly break the pack into clumps. The riders will be encouraged by tens of thousands of spectators as they climb the arid, treeless hulk, but many will be struggling to survive.

The climbs become somewhat milder over the next two stages, but on Saturday, July 16, the first day in the Pyrenees, the racers will again ascend two brutal peaks, the Port-de-Pailhéres and Ax-3 Domaines, over a horrifying 220 kilometers. This is the Tour's longest day, but it is merely a preview for stage 15. Though the Tourmalet (where Octave Lapize shouted "Assassins!" at race officials in 1910) isn't included in 2005, stage 15 makes up for that loss by covering six of the Pyrenees' most fabled passes. If you're only going to pay attention to one Tour stage in 2005, this is it—smart money says that the race may be decided along these six climbs.

CHAPTER 7

Tour de France Confidential

"In the old days, Hugo Koblet chased after women as avidly as he went after the day's yellow jersey, Gino Bartali smoked cigarettes under his biggest rival Coppi's nose and Jacques Anquetil rarely went anywhere without Janine, his platinum blonde. . . ."

—PHILIPPE BRUNEL, JOURNALIST FOR *L'EQUIPE*, WRITING IN *AN INTIMATE PORTRAIT OF THE TOUR DE FRANCE*

The biggest secret of the Tour at last entered the realm of the totally, painfully known on July 8, 1998, three days before the riders were to assemble in Dublin for an international prologue to begin the race. Willy Voet, soigneur for Team Festina, whose stars included Richard Virenque, was stopped by customs as he exited France. In his car was a cache of more than 400 capsules of drugs, including steroids, stimulants, and growth hormones. Tension built over the next few weeks as the racers anxiously made their way along the route. On July 17, with Voet in jail, French police questioned Festina officials, who admitted what everybody suspected: The team was using banned substances to gain an edge in the world's toughest sporting event. Team Festina was thrown out of the race, but the story wasn't over.

What happened next almost destroyed the Tour de France. In Lyon, local police arrested nine Festina riders. Alex Zülle, a Swiss rider for Festina, described his arrest: "In the beginning the officials in Lyons were friendly. But on Thursday evening the horror show began. I was put in an isolation cell and had to strip naked. I had to give up my belt, shoes, even my glasses. They inspected every body cavity. The night was bad, the bed was dirty and it stank. The next morning they confronted me with the compromising documents they had found. They said they were used to seeing hardened criminals in the chair I was sitting on. But is that what we are? I wanted out of that hellhole, so I confessed." Eight other Festina riders admitted drug use.

Police were soon raiding other team facilities. On July 24, with nine stages left to run, racers refused to ride, staging a two-hour strike that left the Tour poised on a precipice. The riders were protesting what they saw as heavy-handed tactics. All concerned were aware that French law bans the use of performance-enhancing drugs in professional sports; it wasn't that, but something deeper. The very condition that makes the Tour a public event—that it unfolds on city streets and village lanes—brought it under the jurisdiction of every local gendarmerie on the route. To the racers, the searches were random, humiliating, and beyond what the investigation seemed to require

Bike racing has become the most tested sport on the planet, with invasive procedures that no U.S. athlete would tolerate.

(imagine Chicago police marching the New York Mets off Wrigley Field to test for steroids). Yes, they'd committed illegal acts. But while it was no excuse to claim that the use of banned substances was virtually a tradition in the Tour, the fact remained that from the beginning, racers have ingested everything from brandy and peppermint to strychnine, cocaine, and nitroglycerine. Nobody ever believed that these were crimes equivalent to street-level narcotics offenses.

Colombia's Fabio Parra led a protest against dope-test rulings that delayed the start of the 20th stage of the 1988 Tour de France.

The "convicts of the road" suddenly were real prisoners. Only Virenque and one teammate persisted in their denials. On July 29, racers staged another protest. In response, Tour officials cancelled that day's Alpine stage. By then, six teams had dropped out in protest of the continuing police actions. Only Marco Pantani's stellar performance in the mountains, setting a new record for the ascent of Alpe d'Huez, saved the Tour that year. Pedaling with an intensity and passion that brought to mind Fausto Coppi, Pantani was awarded the yellow jersey in Paris. However, fewer than 100 riders finished the race.

After–Effects The Tour was in crisis. Race director Jean-Marie Leblanc promised reform and, the next year, implemented one of the most rigorous testing regimes in sports. But the aftermath of the Festina affair lingered for years. It certainly affected Lance Armstrong, who began his string of victories the following year, in 1999; French journalists, many already put off by what they saw as Armstrong's arrogant demeanor, questioned whether somebody who'd had cancer

Racers' spokesman Bjarne Riis of Denmark confers with Tour de France director Jean-Marie Leblanc about the drug-test protest during the 17th stage of the 1998 race.

could possibly come back to win the Tour without artificial performance enhancers. (In fact, during his cancer treatments Armstrong *had* taken EPO, a synthetic hormone that produces red blood cells and is banned by professional cycling. But because he was out of racing at the time, Armstrong's use of it to rebuild his body during his cancer treatments was entirely legitimate and legal.) Over the next five seasons Armstrong became not just cycling's winningest athlete but, under the race's new drug policy, its most tested one. Now, after every stage ended, the day's yellow jersey holder, as well as several riders picked at random, were shuttled into a waiting trailer for blood and urine samples. Armstrong has never failed a drug test, and Team Postal, which was investigated during the Festina affair, was cleared.

Other riders were not so lucky. When the Festina scandal finally reached court, in October 2000, Richard Virenque confessed. "I took doping substances," he said. "I didn't have a choice. I was the sheep, and if they threw me out of the herd I was finished." Virenque continued, in tears, "In the pack you never use the word 'doping.' You say 'medical help.' You are doped only if you get caught." Virenque received a yearlong ban; he returned in 2002 to win the stage at Mont Ventoux, proving to the world, and especially to Tour officials, that he could ride clean and win.

What about Armstrong? The sniping and questioning died down in 2002 and then, in the wake of his courageous showing in 2003, practically vanished. But in 2004, the issue came roaring back—not because of the Tour, but because of what happened afterwards. Tyler Hamilton, who has always played Luke Skywalker to Armstrong's

Darth Vader, was forced to quit the French classic last year because of a back injury. He redeemed himself a month later by winning a gold medal in the Athens Olympics. Then, disaster struck. As Hamilton dropped out of the Tour of Spain with back problems, word spread that a blood sample taken in Athens had tested positive for an apparent transfusion—indicating that the racer may have "blood doped," a process that adds additional oxygen-carrying capacity to an athlete's circulatory system. A second blood sample taken during the Olympics (riders must always be tested twice, and both samples need to indicate foul play) was unusable due to a laboratory error, meaning that Hamilton couldn't be stripped of his Olympic medal. But two tests of samples given in the Spanish event also came back positive.

Hamilton vigorously denied the charges. And he made a strong case that something was wrong with the new test that was used to screen his blood. The World Anti-Doping Agency and the Union Cycliste Internationale did seem to pursue Hamilton with an angry zeal that didn't quite seem appropriate; both groups seemed more like prosecutors than judges, and the UCI refused to certify Hamilton's team, Phonak, in retaliation for Hamilton's decision to fight the charges. Although no decision had been made in the Hamilton case by late 2004 (it was expected in early 2005), the two sanctioning agencies effectively ended the thirty-four-year-old rider's career before he was given a chance to formally defend himself. Of course, it didn't help that another of Hamilton's Phonak teammates tested positive for the same blood tampering, and a third was banned for taking EPO.

It was not a stellar moment for the Tour, and it raised new questions about Armstrong and the entire professional peloton. Will drugs ever disappear from the Tour? Probably not. The Tour's "cleanliness" has always been a topic of debate. There will always be riders who seek advantage. There will always be new substances and new ways to avoid detection. A bigger question is whether or not these substances should be banned at all, or whether some provision for administering them under medical supervision, for the safety of the riders, should be established. That such a debate even exists may be a bit shocking to Americans, but it is important to remember that Europe is a more permissive place than the U.S.; some coaches point out that the difference between a "banned substance" and a legal "nutritional supplement" is a blurry one at best. Some substances are legal in certain amounts, but cross that line and you're a doper.

Tour organizers and participating teams seem to understand that keeping the race honest is essential to the Tour's global appeal and credibility. Bike racing has become the most tested sport on the planet, with invasive procedures that no U.S. athlete would tolerate. Major league baseball, for example, only last year agreed to serious testing for performance-enhancing drugs, and even the current procedures used in the sport—instituted after several top pros admitted to illegal steroid use—are laughable compared to what professional cyclists undergo. But the lack of due process in the Hamilton case highlights the irony inherent in the sport's drug policy. Bike racers have no union or bargaining entity, so they (and their teams) can be penalized arbitrarily; this is why cycling can rightfully say that no other sport is tougher on illicit performance enhancement. On the other hand, racers like Hamilton can justifiably argue that this toughness, so essential to preserving cycling's reputation, is what can ultimately, and unfairly, end their careers.

Hamilton, for his part, asserts that, whether or not he's banned, he will be in the Tour de France again. If he's forced to take a two-year break, as Richard Virenque was, the American racer says: "I would come back and win the Tour de France, for my sport, for me, for everyone who has believed in me."

Arcane, Written Rules

The Tour also has some unique formal regulations. Riders can lose points or be fined (always in Swiss Francs) for transgressions such as bumping another rider or hanging on to a team car for too long. (You have to have a good reason for the latter, usually that you're being given a boost up to speed after a repair, in which case 100 meters is the limit.) In 2003, fines of 50 to 100 Swiss Francs were levied on riders who failed to sign in at the start of the stage, accepted pushes from spectators, drafted behind team cars, or generally failed to follow the instructions of race officials.

Arcane, *Unwritten* Rules In 2003,

when Lance Armstrong tangled his handlebar in a fan's purse and tumbled to the tarmac as he climbed Luz-Ardiden, the lead riders slowed to allow the fallen yellow jersey holder to catch up. If Jan Ullrich, who was among that group, had attacked instead, he almost certainly would have won the Tour. But that kind of opportunism is unthinkable. "To attack under those circumstances," Ullrich said, "is impossible. That's not how anyone wins the Tour de France." The idea is part of the uniqueness of the event. It also grows from the fact that a three-week race, whose participants virtually live on their bikes, necessitates a social contract that supercedes any written set

Not so lonely at the top: Jan Ullrich and Lance Armstrong shake hands during the final stage of the 2003 Tour de France.

of rules. This contract includes the following, less visible, unofficial customs:

- **Table Manners:** Attempting to gain an advantage during a meal break (in the centralized feed zone, usually designated near the stage's halfway point) is a major taboo. No contending rider would dare, and even one who's not in jersey contention would face ostracism for behaving that way.

- **Home Visits:** If the race passes through a rider's village, the peloton allows that rider to pedal ahead so he can stop and have a traditional glass of Champagne with friends and family. When the pack appears, he rejoins it in the position he left.

- **Vive la France:** If it won't affect the general classification, it is considered good form to allow

1975 Leaders of the pack

(l. to r.): Felice Gimondi of Italy, Bernard Thévenet of France (overall leader), Lucien Van Impe of Belgium (mountain leader), Joop Zoetemelk of the Netherlands, and Eddy Merckx.

a Frenchman to win on Bastille Day. The last French rider to do so was Laurent "Jaja" Jalabert, who took the holiday stage in 2001.

- **Happy Birthday to Me:** If a rider's birthday occurs during the race, the peloton slows down for a moment to congratulate him (again, only if it won't affect the general classification). A drop of Champagne and a bit of cake are sometimes included. The more serious Champagne drinking occurs on the last day's ride into Paris. If the Tour is basically decided, the peloton turns into a parade, at least until it reaches the Champs-Élysées, when the power goes back on for ten breakneck circuits.

Victor Hugo Peña of the U.S. Postal Team being weighed for a birthday gift of his weight in Champagne in 2003.

- **Etiquette de la Toilette:** Riders do have to relieve themselves during the Tour. Attacking when a race leader has stopped to answer nature's call is a flagrant breach of custom. The Tour also features bathroom breaks organized en masse. Usually, a senior rider will call for a group rest stop, and if you need to go, you'd better do it. If stopping is impossible and nature not only calls but screams, riders do it on the fly, usually with a teammate or two pushing him along as he conducts one of bike racing's most delicate maneuvers. Of course, you'll never see these moments on television: The code of chivalry extends to the media as well.

- **Exceptions to the Rules:** In 2003 Frenchman Sylvain Chavanel led most of the day and, on the final climb up Luz-Ardiden, held a narrow lead as the dramatic fight for the overall unfolded lower down. Armstrong, as everybody knows, rode like a man possessed after his fall, and caught Chavanel near the finish line. Since the Frenchman was no threat to Armstrong's overall position, normal etiquette would dictate that the Texan let the rider who'd led the race so long take a well-earned stage win. But since the 2003 Tour was so close, Armstrong needed the 20-second time bonus awarded to the daily winner. Chavanel knew and understood this. Armstrong acknowledged Chavanel's consideration with a traditional gesture of contrition, touching his rival's shoulder as he passed.

Dough   Riders' salaries can dip as low as $20,000, although $180,000 is much closer to the average today for a Tour rider (which is still marginal compared to other sports). Tour racers on a winning team receive a huge bonus. The race's total purse goes up every year. In 2004 it was $3 million. Of that, about $400,000 goes to the yellow jersey holder, who shares it with his team. The rest is distributed throughout the race to each day's top sprinters, first twenty-five finishers, and anyone wearing one of the colored jerseys.

Swag   Nobody goes home empty-handed from the Tour de France. The term for the freebies tossed into the crowd from the sponsor vehicles in *la Caravane* is "swag." For the past several years the most-distributed Tour knick-knacks have been tiny bags of gummy bears. Haribo, the European confectionary giant that makes them, estimates that more than two million packets of candy are hurled each year. Some of the souvenirs are even better: caps and T-shirts, banners and posters, and, perhaps best of all on brutally hot days, cold

If a rider's birthday occurs during the race, the peloton slows down for a moment to congratulate him. A drop of Champagne and a bit of cake are sometimes included.

beverages and dousing spray from high-powered hoses, courtesy of the event's soft-drink sponsors.

Fanatics With the possible exception of Linda Armstrong, Lance's mother, the biggest and certainly most conspicuous Tour fan is Didi Senft, also known as "Devil Man." This oversize German, who leads guests on tours of the Tour, can be seen at nearly every stage, as well as on television, prancing in crimson garb complete with horns, tail, and pitchfork. Other personalities include spectators who show up in full team kit— looking every inch the pro, with replica everything from head to toe (bike included); naked fans (there are always a few); and the Italian fans known as *Tifosi*. These are bike racing's most partisan boosters. Although they don't riot, as soccer fans do, you can tell you've seen one when an Italian rider passes and the spectator running alongside him wears a look on his face that com-

A free bag of gummy bears helps sweeten the experience of waiting for the riders to pass.

bines ecstasy with a sort of awestruck hysteria (the type usually reserved for those who see the face of God).

Other Jerseys, Other Prizes The best rider under age twenty-five receives the white jersey. In 2004, that award went to the Russian Vladimir Karpets. The sprinter's green jersey went to Robbie McEwen, the powerful Australian. And Richard Virenque, in his final Tour, not only won a record seventh King of the Mountains jersey, but also the non-jersey combativity award, given to the most aggressive rider. (The reason there's no combativity jersey is simple: The winner would become the target of every other aggressive rider, turning the whole thing into a chaotic revolving door. Instead, the racer leading in aggressiveness points is given red rider numbers, instead of the traditional white—guaranteeing that only *some* of the other aggressive riders will start gunning for him.)

Citrus Citations The French press presents a pair of awards to riders. *Le citron*, the lemon, goes to the least cooperative rider. Armstrong's early, rocky relationship with Gallic journalists earned him that "honor" in 2001. By 2003 Armstrong had turned the tables; by making sure he appeared nearly every day on French television, speaking the language, he earned the race's other media homage: *l'orange*, or orange prize, for most cooperative rider.

Banned Bikes The highest-profile forbidden objects in a recent Tour were bikes that U.S. manufacturer Cannondale supplied for Team Saeco (an Italian manufacturer of coffee makers). Official regulations say a tour machine can't weigh less than 6.8 kilograms (14.99 pounds), but the

Cannondales weighed in at just a hair under that. In order to use the Cannondales, team officials added weights. Of course, they didn't have to add much, and a few people suggested that the whole thing was a publicity stunt. Team officials denied it, although that failed to explain why so many T-shirts and jerseys appeared with the words "Legalize My Cannondale!" on them.

Cold Case   The biggest unsolved mystery of the Tour concerns the death of Ottavio Bottecchia, who in 1924 became the first Italian to win the Tour de France. On June 14, 1927, he was found, on a training ride, bloodied and unconscious, propped against a tree, by the side of the road. His bike was undamaged and neatly arranged beside him. The racer was taken to a local church, where he died. At first the explanation was that a local farmer, enraged that the racer was picking grapes, had killed him—but that made no sense—grapes aren't in season at that time of year. More likely, Bottecchia, a socialist and national hero, was seen as a threat to the fascism that had begun rising in Italy around that time. Over the years, two more bits of information emerged. As he was dying after being stabbed, an Italian mobster confessed to the killing but didn't live to explain the reason for it. In 1973 the parish priest who'd given Bottecchia his last rites said local Fascists committed the crime. Both explanations raised as many questions as answers, and the murder of the first great Italian Tour champion remains officially unsolved.

CHAPTER 8

Audience Participation

"It is the equivalent of the Super Bowl, but every day for twenty-three days. . . . I doubt there is any sporting equivalent to compare it to."

—Phil Liggett, the English-language "voice" of the Tour

Inventory of Mont Ventoux, southern France, July 21, 2002: Tens of thousands of folding chairs line the side of the road, all occupied by people who rightly believe that red wine is best if you drink it before eight in the morning. The road is patrolled by a fleet of trucks selling hats and newspapers and T-shirts and warm drinks under a sign marked "cold drinks." They all play loud music and their horns all seem to be stuck in mid-blare. Graffiti is scrawled across

Say *fromage*.

the macadam in chalk, offering thanks to Laurent Jalabert, a retiring French veteran. And bike riders by the thousands, on old racers, mountain machines, three-speeds, and tandems, pedal past wannabes, kids, little old ladies, and folks with missing limbs, all ascending through fifty switchbacks toward a broiling summit.

The 200 racers who make up this year's Tour de France are due late in the afternoon. But to anyone pedaling Ventoux in the morning, the Tour has already arrived—especially as each of the spectators, some of whom have been waiting for days, clap them on the back, applaud, and offer encouragement *"Courage! Courage!"*—as they ascend. For those not pedaling? It's a splendid way to picnic while waiting for the most thrilling parade on earth to appear.

There are several ways to see the Tour in person, and you should make it a point to do at least one of them, because—in addition to putting you into joyously frenzied scenes like the one above—it will pretty much change your life. (It won't make you a better person, just a deeper one, not unlike the effect of gazing at the ceiling of the Sistine Chapel.) You'll join a whopping, three-week-long tailgate party that puts any single-day U.S. event to shame: millions of spectators, better food, as much wine as beer, and when the athletes pass, the chance to actually see their faces. If you visit from America, nothing can prepare you for the insanity, the power, and the sheer speed of the peloton as it passes. It is absolutely guaranteed that you will be swept away by the excitement; that you will become addicted; and that for the rest of your life you'll know exactly what you'll be doing every July.

Some General Advice Want to add the Tour to your European vacation? First figure out when and where. Go to the Tour's official

Web site, download a day-to-day schedule, and pick the days you want to watch. The key tip for Tour spectators is, get yourself into viewing position early. The major stages—the Alps, the Pyrenees, and the final run down the Champs-Élysées—are pretty much like outdoor rock festivals: If you want the good spots, you need to camp out. Gendarmes close some of the major climbs to car traffic a day before the stage. Consider arriving a day early and sending one member of your group with lots of blankets and folding chairs; he or she can take a car, set up, and spend the night. You should arrive at least four hours prior to the time the racers are expected to pass (check out *L'Equipe*, the French sports daily, which lists a full schedule of predicted arrival times at various points along the course). At some point, the route closes even to foot traffic.

What about accommodations? The best places to stay are the small cottages, hotels, and chalets in the towns along the route. For climbing days,

Please pass the peloton.

try to get as close to the mountain as possible. Many accommodations are sold out in advance, so another option is to base yourself in a nearby city. Chamonix and Grenoble are about an hour or two from most of the Tour's Alpine spots, and Lourdes is about the same distance from the Pyrenees. In Paris, try to get a hotel room within walking distance of the Champs-Élysées, where the action is.

Just Watching

You've got three choices of venue: the villages, the mountains, and Paris. The village experience is the most low-key—there are fewer spectators, and you're really just waiting for the riders to flash by for a minute or two. This is an ideal way to add a few days of Tour watching to a vacation in the French countryside. The best strategy is park yourself in a small town on the Tour route, find a nice spot on the side of the road, and take a picnic and a good book. Work on your tan until you hear the helicopters. Or, you can find a café and enjoy a leisurely wait while sipping a café au lait and watching the race progress on television. You'll know the riders are close when the caravan passes and helicopters thunder above you. You'll know the riders are *really* close, however, when a sweaty odor begins to fill the air. Yes, the peloton smells—why wouldn't it, after all those miles and all that perspiration?

The mountains present a greater logistical challenge for spectators. Rolling closures are enforced on most routes, often randomly by enthusiastic gendarmes. If you'd like to drive to a high-altitude vantage point, arrive at least a day before (and be prepared for your own grueling descent after the stage, when every single vehicle

The Tour de France leaves Albi in 1953.

on the hill attempts to crawl home at the same time). Much better—and truer to the spirit of the race—is getting to your spot under your own steam. You can walk, or use a bike, to make your way uphill on the day of the stage. Getting as high up as possible is worth the effort (leave in the morning, go slow, drink water) because you can watch the

action below you as it unfolds. Don't forget a blanket to lie on, a few baguettes, some cheese, and a bottle of wine.

Finally there's Paris. If the Tour is like twenty Super Bowls, the final day on the Champs-Élysées is like half a dozen Oscars Parties. The racers pedal through the streets of Paris, arriving on the Champs-Élysées for ten circuits of 5 kilometers

The American presence, and reverence, is growing.

Fans wave from a pizzeria on wheels as the peloton slices by in 1995.

Front-row seats, Neufchatel en Bray, 1988

each, but the crowds arrive long before that, staking out viewing spots along the main avenue, some as early as the evening before. Why? Because even though the final stage is supposed to be noncompetitive, those ten circuits are amazing. It isn't just that the riders go faster and faster, round and round, so you feel like you're watching a Formula One race. It's that all this speed and action is in your face, not to mention the caravan, which—after three weeks of travel—has gone giddily punch-drunk. By 1 P.M., every spectator is sweltering in the intense heat as the caravan arrives with its scantily clad hostesses representing bottled-water companies, who throw candy and lewdly squirt parched fans with fire hoses. A series of other vehicles, combining elements of Macy's parade floats and Halloween, come honking and zigzagging along the wide boulevard, some carrying oompah bands. Everybody's ready for some excitement.

But the best moment of all is when the riders are almost on the famed boulevard. Suddenly, there's total quiet. Then, there's a clatter, amplified by the canyon of the street and by the presence of the entire pack now riding together. It is almost scary: nearly 150 riders, whizzing by with an audible snap—the roaring sound of air being pushed through more than 5,000 spokes.

Riding the Tour A more intense way to experience the Tour is to follow it for several days on a bike. You pedal the choicest parts of the Tour's most legendary stages and use your excursions to secure a personal skybox along the side of the road. You can make the rides as easy or as hard as you want: Choose flat days, small segments of the mountains, or go for major mileage by combining key Tour summits. You can plan a trip like this on your own (buy Lonely Planet's *Cycling France,* which includes a chapter on riding

Tour group (ies).

during the Tour; $19.99, www.lonelyplanet.com)
or—as most folks do—try a prepackaged version.
Catered visits last from four days to two weeks,
with a dozen or so riders moving from town to
town, pedaling along routes pre-scouted by your
tour leaders. Most of the trips include a "sag
wagon," your group's own version of the broom
wagon, though probably loaded with more, and
less healthy, snacks. The amount of actual Tour
viewing you get on these trips varies (some are
more for general sightseers, with a little Tour de
France mixed in), so make sure you check in
advance. Some of the most popular shadow trips
are offered by Backroads, the world's largest bike
touring company, which offers about a dozen packages, of varying lengths and degrees of difficulty.
Prices start at about $3,000. Call (800) 462-2848
or go to www.backroads.com.

Other American companies offering Tour
packages include VéloSport Vacations—a little
less pricey, with itineraries geared toward
the serious Tour enthusiast, (800) 988-9833;
www.velovacations.com. If you want to ride with
the pros, book Trek Travel's "Behind the Scenes"
trip; you get to meet the Discovery team. Trek also
offers several other Tour packages, (866) 464-8735;
www.trektravel.com. If joining busloads of Brits
sounds appealing, check out the world's biggest
operator of Tour de France holidays, Britain's
Graham Baxter Sporting Tours. Baxter's lower-
priced tours operate out of a fleet of Greyhound-size
coaches and carry hundreds of cycling-crazed
vacationers at a time. The company offers special
visits for noncyclists, as well as packages for folks
who want to ride, making the Baxter tours good
for mixed groups (www.sportingtours.co.uk).

If you want to truly experience what it's like to
ride the Tour—rather than just watch—consider
entering the official *l'Étape du Tour,* a huge, public

bike ride held on a single day during every tour. The Étape attracts up to 10,000 riders from around the world; they generally pedal the length of an entire Tour stage, but shorter options are possible. Although the Étape is supposed to be a noncompetitive fun ride, at the front of the pack it quickly degenenerates—or accelerates—into breakneck competition. Hang out in the back and you'll do fine. This year's Étape, to be held on July 11, travels between Mourenx and Pau, covering an ambitious 178 kilometers. Registration is required: http://www.letapedutour.com/2005/us/index.htm.

Another way to immerse yourself in French bike culture is to spend a few extra days in Paris before or after the final stage. Nearly every city has a standard bike route that riders—usually of all shapes and sizes—follow on Saturday. In Los Angeles, folks pedal circuits around the Rose

In 1994, Armand De Las Cuevas, Miguel Indurain, and Richard Virenque got encouragement—perhaps too much—as they climbed Mont Ventoux.

Bowl. In New York, it's Central Park. In Paris, it's the Bois de Boulogne, a vast, wooded park on the east side of town. The route is a 4-kilometer circle around l'Hippodrome de Longchamp, a horse-racing track, and it attracts all kinds: wannabes, once-weres, club riders, and plenty of Stomachs (old-time racers, still wearing their team jerseys, which are stretched tight by their larger bellies). There's one ride on Saturday afternoon, and another on Sunday.

CHAPTER 9

Bob Roll's Unauthorized, Unexpurgated Tour de France Alphabet

In which the author explains the ABCs of it all.

Alpe d'Huez Twenty-one switchbacks, 600 meters of climbing. From 1949, when Fausto Coppi won the Tour's first ascent of this now legendary uphill, to LeMond's battle with Bernard Hinault in 1986, to its role as the launch pad for Lance Armstrong's most brilliant tour moment, this is where angels climb—in a trance of pain. No single ride more defines the Tour de France.

Bikes Gear for the regular road stages has remained virtually unchanged since the first tour in 1903. Where the technological advantages of the modern world have crept in is on the time trial machines. Idaho's Boone Lennon brought the ski-racing position, with aerodynamic handlebars, to the Tour in 1989, and with that stroke of

genius precipitated the greatest comeback in the
history of the sport: Greg LeMond overcoming a
50-second deficit to win the Tour by just 8 seconds
over Laurent Fignon. How significant are aerodynamics? Today, a middle-of-the-pack Tour rider
maintains an average speed of 6 kilometers per
hour faster than Eddy Merckx, the 1960s and
1970s legend who is considered the greatest bike
racer of all time.

Coppi They called Fausto Coppi "Il
Campionissimo," the champion of champions.
During World War II, he had spent six years as a
prisoner of war in Tunisia. His postwar rivalry with
Gino Bartali (Bartali won in 1948, Coppi the next
year) single-handedly rescued the Italian people
from the devastation of that conflict. Coppi was a
beautiful human being, and in Italy he's revered
with an apostolic devotion. There has never been a

greater example of a country's virtue than Coppi—
he was a simple peasant who helped the people
understand that where there's life, there's hope.

Devil Take the Hindmost What makes
the Tour so hard? It's very simple: It's the time
limit. Each rider has to finish within a specified
percentage of the stage winner's total, every day
of the tour. What that means is that, unlike climbing mountains or doing the Ironman, if you're not
within 10 percent or so of the fastest guy *every
single day,* you're going home in a body bag. That
means even the *lanterne rouge,* the man in last
place, is exceptional.

Electronics More than any single advance,
the electronic earpiece that connects riders to
team managers has changed the tactical landscape of cycling. The team manager can get the
time gaps and composition of any breakaway on a
moment-to-moment basis, and can even watch the
break's progress on TV and report to his rider
exactly the level of effort they need in order to
contain it. Americans were the first to use two-
way radios. The most famous use was in 1999,
stage 8, when U.S. Postal race director Johan
Bruyneel screamed, "Attack! Now!" to Armstrong,
who took the advice and went on to a powerful
stage win. Now every team uses radio communi-
cations, as well as real-time data analysis (stored
on laptops in the team cars, and gathered from
live television feeds) to determine when to make
a move, and when to counter the opposition's.

Racers also use telemetric tracking devices to
measure their speed and to transmit finish-line
results to race officials (creating moderate con-
fusion when, in the event of a breakdown, a team
leader switches bikes with a *domestique*). Bringing
the tour to more than 500 million viewers around

Electronic earpieces brought the Tour de France into the Information Age.

the world is also a technological marvel; the French take it seriously, providing a single, live feed to the entire planet; an AWACS-like reconnaissance aircraft follows the peloton, so images can be bounced off it to international satellites without interference from the mountains or crowds.

French *Domestique* is a misunderstood term in America. It doesn't mean "maid" or "servant." A *domestique* is a racer who supports a team leader by dropping back for water, providing a wind buffer, and chasing rival teams in order to tire them out. Like *peloton* and *echelon*, it's one of the words that just can't be explained better in another language. Not only is the Tour the perfect stage race, but the French language is the most compelling and accurate way to explain the Tour, and the entire sport of cycling.

Grand Tours   There are three Grand Tours: the Giro d'Italia, the Vuelta a España, and the big daddy of them all, the Tour de France. The Tour is biggest because the French have the most intense love, a nonpatriotic devotion to athletic prowess. It doesn't matter what country you're from—they love Muhammad Ali as much as they love Jean-Claude Killy. Geographically, France is the perfect venue for a three-week bike race. It makes a nearly perfect circle, and the geography always assures that the strongest man will prevail. That first week on windy, flat northern roads, the second and third in the Alps and Pyrenees, and the final promenade into Paris—all a perfect *grande boucle,* or great loop.

Haribo   The maker of gummy bears is just one of the tour's major sponsors. Others include Nestlè, Coke, Michelin, and Kawasaki—and caravan vehicles range from simple vans with logos to high-speed parade floats, shaped like cakes, tires, or giant cans of soda. The total caravan comprises more than 200 vehicles—sponsor trucks, team cars, official and press vehicles—and snakes for five miles, taking up to an hour to pass spectators on the course while handing out 11 million pieces of swag. (The caravan is the carrot in front of the donkey. Make no mistake about the racers; they may be on a spiritual quest in this most working-class of sports, but every one of them also wants to ensure that *he* never has to work a day in his life.) Hundreds of thousands of fans line the asphalt during the tour's more popular stages. Although they get only a fleeting glimpse of the pack as it flies by, the swag is endless: caps, T-shirts, and especially candy are crowd favorites.

Ivan Since the fall of Communism, there's been a huge migration of riders from Eastern Bloc countries, none of whom ever had a chance to make money until they were able to participate in the classics. They bring an intense work ethic to the peloton. When somebody like Jan Ullrich, who came from East Germany, puts the hammer down, forget it. They've helped internationalize the sport, making it a unifying force for Europe.

Jean-Marie Leblanc Director of the Tour de France, and the event's aristocrat. He single-handedly dragged the race out of the dark ages, away from the Byzantine madness and bureaucratic mire of provincial Franco-insanity, and in doing so he has created the single most beautiful athletic contest in the world. Not too long ago, the tour was a very French affair. Now it's as international as the soccer World Cup and the Olympics. (He's still capable of being imperious, though: Witness 2003's Cipollini fiasco, in which a prideful difference of opinion between the best sprinter in cycling and Leblanc kept Cipollini out of the race. The rift appears to have been mended.)

King of the Mountains When the public sees a superstar like Lance Armstrong dying like an animal on a hill climb, people are quickly disabused of the notion that these are privileged people having a grand time. Nobody in the race can escape the suffering—and the place where that's most obvious is in the mountains. The list of Tour de France King of the Mountains winners is a pantheon of martyred warriors.

Lance There's never been a specimen quite as well adapted to the sport of cycling, nor has any athlete been as focused on that one race in the history of the sport. Lance is a very nice guy, and

the most loyal friend you could ever dream of
having—but woe be to his enemies. He won't rest
until he scatters their ashes across the four cor-
ners of the cycling globe. If you were handed an
ember of coal, you'd drop it. Lance would hold on.

*M*usette The feed bag that the riders grab
during the long stages. In the old days it was filled
with sandwiches, cakes, and water bottles. Today
it consists of energy bars and concentrated glucose drinks. The food in today's musettes is more
sterile—the riders don't get sick as much. In the
old days, there was a constant level of bacterial
and viral debilitation.

**I don't brake
for food:** Riders
grab *musettes* on
their way through
town in 1956.

Night The ritual has stayed the same since the beginning of the tour. After the stage finishes, you are shuttled to your hotel, where you take off your racing kit and put it in the sink. You clean your jersey and shorts, take a shower, get a massage, eat dinner, then go to bed. You don't sleep. You're too exhausted and overstimulated. The screaming fans, hair-raising descents, and backbreaking climbs disrupt even the slightest possibility of rest. But the nighttime ritual keeps you grounded. It's almost as soothing and restful as eight hours of dead-to-the-world shuteye.

Over the Limit Cycling is the only sport that is full of true crime and true punishment. Any other pro sport is smart enough to realize that continual drug scandals would put them out of business, so they don't bother to pursue the matter. Baseball players are like, "Drug testing? We think not." But cycling isn't a stadium sport. Riders aren't in a controlled environment; they're riding down your street, which gives the cop on the beat jurisdiction over them! You can't have a peloton of drug-crazed psychopaths flying through your neighborhood, so bike racing has become something of a moving police lineup. And yes, the stress and drugs and competition take five years off a rider's life, but there's no estimating what kind of mischief these guys would have gotten into if they hadn't become bike racers.

Peloton The peloton—pack—tends to stay together on the flats because drafting, sitting behind the rider in front, requires 30 percent less effort than leading. But when the race gets to the mountains and gravity becomes the enemy, that figure drops to less than 5 percent, and you see the group split up. Watching the peloton, with its bright colors and phenomenal speed—up to 65

The power of
the pack

kilometers (40 mi) per hour—is one of the most
beautiful spectacles in sport, and the aerodynamics
within the peloton are what separates cycling from
any other endurance event. Without a team that
knows how to relay him to the mountains, keeping
him out of the wind and safe near the front of the
pack, not even Lance could win the Tour.

Quitting The last thing you want to do is
drop out of the Tour de France. Of all sports,
cycling provides us with the most potent allegory
of life, so dropping out is almost like dying. That's
why you see men turn themselves inside out just
to finish the event—even when they have no
chance of winning, not even one stage, or even
a single time trial. The other side of the Tour's
trance of pain is quitting, and you do not ever
want to go there.

Rivals The only way to beat Lance is to not get him mad at you. You've got to be so nice and demure and retiring that he doesn't even realize you're in the race. So far, this has proved impossible.

Soigneur Another nearly untranslatable French term. He's more than just the trainer—he's the guy who cooks meals, prepares the *musette,* and gives massages. A good *soigneur* listens to the litany of fatigue-induced laments and complaints, night after night, and offers nothing but encouragement. Recriminations and criticism are the job of the team manager.

T-Mobile If any team has a chance at beating Discovery and Lance Armstrong, it's this German-based squad, which includes Ullrich and Andreas Klöden, who finished fourth and second in 2004, respectively. More than any other team, T-Mobile is in a position to frustrate Team

Jan Ullrich:
What's love got to do with it?

Discovery's efforts to capture for Armstrong a record seventh victory.

Ullrich Armstrong's most gifted rival, a product of the East German athletic juggernaut—and probably the most successful ever to emerge from that program. He's the perfect example of a system that plucks children from school and turns them into machines. Jan pedals not out of love of the sport, but out of a sense of obligation. Based on physiology, he should have won five tours by now—but because of Ullrich's arrested development at the hands of a vanquished government system, Armstrong has always been able to defeat him. And not only because Lance loves to race; the American also has a genuine and innocent love of riding his bike every single day. In 2004, Ullrich faltered badly. Big question for 2005: Can Ullrich muster the heart to win?

Victory What does it take to win? There's a purely physical requirement—you have to be a special athlete, with a complicated combination of slow and fast twitch muscles, effective lactic acid production, and a huge cardiovascular system. At least half the field meets these requirements, but only one man can win, and that's where the psychological requirement comes in. You have to enjoy hurting yourself as much as you enjoy hurting your rivals. Not many people are willing to do that. As a matter of fact, there's only one per year.

Worry Being a bike racer is like being a Delta blues singer—worry and trouble are the only things on your mind. There's so much worrying in the Tour that you reach a state of frenzy. You're turned into a zombie who worries about how much you sleep, talk, stand up, sit down, how much you eat or drink, how much your bike

weighs, how much money you're making.
Successful worry management is one of the
things that makes Tour champions.

X-Men The Europeans have 100 years of
experience on us, and there may be a lot more of
them in the Tour, but what we Americans lack in
numbers, we make up in vitality. While we don't
enjoy the tradition of decades of racing, we're also
not as beholden to that tradition. The U.S. has
four or five guys in the race each year, and
Americans have won seven of the last fifteen
Tours. Our distance from the Tour's traditions
frees us to try new methods, new technologies—
and that has led to our current dominance.

Yellow The Golden Fleece. No team is allowed
to sport predominantly yellow uniforms or jerseys
because it would draw attention—and honor—
away from the garb of the race leader. When you
wear *le maillot jaune*, everyone knows *you're the
one*. There's a basic human desire to be recog-
nized by our peers, and the yellow jersey is the
most graphic evidence of that in sports. Wearing
it—even for one day—is the most significant
moment in a bike racer's life. He'll forever be
known as a man who led the Tour de France.
Actually *winning* the yellow jersey changes you
in ways you never imagined. You give up a portion
of your own life. There will always be a part of you
that belongs to the collective consciousness, to
hope, to the triumph over adversity that winning
the Tour de France represents. That's the loss, and
that's the benefit.

Zen For every guy in the tour, there comes a
point when he doesn't feel physically capable of
finishing. At that moment the race becomes spiritual. The moment he surmounts his weakness

changes his life. In my first Tour, I made a conscious decision to put no limits on the amount of suffering I'd endure. I didn't sleep. The ceiling started to drip blood and the saints came out of the walls, sat on my bed, and talked to me. I went from weighing 165 pounds, with 4 percent body fat, to 148 pounds at the finish. By the time it was over, I felt like a 72-year-old. But I finished. And it changed me forever.

1962 The beloved Raymond Poulidor rides his first Tour. His courage and persistence win the hearts of French fans, but in 14 tries, he'll never win, coming in second five times and third five times, and spending not a single day in the yellow jersey.

1964 Anquetil wins a record fifth Tour (he also wins the Giro d'Italia in 1964).

1965 With Anquetil out of the race, Poulidor's chance to win arrives at last—but he's beaten by Italian phenom Felice Gimondi.

1966 Tour organizers hold their first surprise doping tests. The riders stage a brief protest strike.

1967 Tom Simpson, the first Briton to wear the Tour's yellow jersey (stage 2, 1962), collapses and dies just beneath the summit of Mont Ventoux. Drugs are implicated.

1969 Eddy Merckx—the Cannibal— enters his first Tour de France and destroys the field, outpacing his rival by almost 8 minutes on a single day in the Pyrenees, and going on to take the first of his five tour victories.

1971 In a strategy similar to the one employed by Lance Armstrong's rivals 32 years later, Merckx's competitors band together in an attempt to attack and exhaust the Belgian superstar. Unlike 2003, the tactic is effective, and Spaniard Luis Ocaña looks like he might win the race until he crashes in the Pyrenees and has to withdraw. Merckx, now leading, refuses to wear the yellow jersey the next day, but winds up with his third consecutive Tour victory in Paris a few days later.

1973 Merckx skips the Tour, and Luis Ocaña finally wins.

1975 Merckx goes for his record sixth Tour yellow. While he's climbing the Puy-de-Dôme, a French spectator punches him in the kidney. Bernard Thévenet wins the race; Merckx's career Tour victories total ends at five as he finishes second, 2:47 behind Thevenet. The Tour's finish line, for the first time, is the Champs-Élysées.

1978 Bernard Hinault, nicknamed "The Badger" for his tenacity, takes the first of his five Tour wins. Hinault also leads a rider strike to protest the exhausting policy of splitting stages, effectively holding two races in a single day, as a way for Tour organizers to earn extra entry fees from sponsoring towns. The action is successful, and the practice is halted.

1980 Hinault withdraws from the Tour due to a knee injury. The press speculates that his career is over.

1981 A healthy Hinault returns to the Tour and utterly dominates. Jonathan Boyer becomes the first American to race in the Tour, finishing 32nd.

1982 Hinault wins the Tour and the Giro d'Italia.

1983 An injured Hinault doesn't start the Tour, leaving Laurent Fignon—a virtual unknown with a bookish look (due to his glasses)—to win the race.

1985 Hinault, desperate to win his fifth Tour, battles Fignon and his own young teammate, Greg LeMond. LeMond helps his team leader take the general classification. "I will do whatever I can to help Greg win next year," a grateful Hinault tells the press. LeMond becomes the first American to win a Tour stage.

1986 Hinault decides to go for his sixth jersey win. LeMond accuses the Frenchman of breaking his promise, to which Hinault replies, "I will help you only if you prove yourself worthy of the yellow jersey." Hinault then goes on to lead the race until LeMond drops him in the Alps. The two summit Alpe d'Huez, hand in hand. The torch is passed, and Greg LeMond becomes the first American to win the Tour. It is a banner year for the USA: Besides LeMond, Davis Phinney wins a stage and team member Alex Stieda wears the yellow jersey early in the race. This is also Bob Roll's first Tour. All but LeMond ride for the first American team ever to enter the race, Team 7-Eleven, also known as the Slurpees.

1987 Greg LeMond is shot by his brother-in-law in a hunting accident. He loses 75 percent of his blood, and nearly dies. Whether he'll ever return to bike racing is questionable.

1987 Stephen Roche becomes the first Irishman to win the Tour de France.

1989 LeMond's amazing comeback, in a thrilling duel with Laurent Fignon. It takes a climactic time trial on the streets of Paris—it's the Tour's last day—for LeMond to complete his victory, edging a disbelieving and tearful Fignon by 8 seconds, the smallest winning margin in Tour history. LeMond's winning time makes for the fastest stage ever, at 54.55 kilometers per hour.

1989 Current Tour director Jean-Marie Leblanc takes over. He's largely credited with turning the race into a global sporting event.

1990 LeMond wins again.

1991 Miguel Indurain, the towering Spaniard, wins the first of his five Tours. Indurain is a cool and calculating rider, generating little excitement but dominating in his calmness.

1992 Despite a strong challenge by the stylish and passionate Italian Claudio Chiappucci, Indurain wins again, turning in an astonishing time trial performance in stage 19 and winning by more than 3 minutes. In his Tour de France career, Indurain will win only one non-time trial event.

1993 Lance Armstrong wins his first Tour de France stage but fails to complete the race.

1994 Riders once again employ an "all against one" tactic, but it fails to rattle Indurain, who goes on to win his fourth Tour.

1995 Indurain wins his fifth and final Tour in a race darkened by the death of Fabio Casartelli, the 1992 Olympic gold medalist, who crashes on a Pyrenean descent. After a one-stage neutralization in his memory, Casartelli's American teammate, Lance Armstrong, races stage 18 in tribute to his friend, and wins. Armstrong completes the Tour de France for the first time, 36th overall.

1996 Lance Armstrong is diagnosed with testicular cancer; the disease has spread throughout his body, and his odds of survival are assessed at 40 percent.

1997 Jan Ullrich becomes the first German to win the Tour de France.

His mountaintop sprint to the finish line at Andorre-Arcalis in the Pyrenees destroys the field.

1998 The Festina Affair. One team is discovered using drugs, setting off a domino effect that will ultimately see six squads leave the Tour. Italian climber Marco Pantani wins a race tainted by scandal, becoming the first Italian to do so in over 30 years.

1998 Armstrong, pronounced cancer-free, begins returning to form but doesn't race the Tour.

1999 Armstrong wins his first Tour, dominating in both the mountains and time trials. The victory is the first for a U.S.-based team, as well as the first time an American-made bike (and a bike with a Japanese drivetrain) have ever won the Tour. It is also the first tour in over 70 years in which a French rider fails to win a stage.

2000 Skeptics noted that in 1999 Armstrong had beaten a field that included neither Pantani nor Ullrich. In 2000, with both those rivals participating, Armstrong wins again. Race officials, admitting there is currently no effective test for the presence of EPO, a red blood cell booster he had been taking to counteract his chemotherapy, begin the practice of freezing urine samples for future analysis.

2001 Most memorable moment: Armstrong's "bluff" on Alpe d'Huez,

when he feigns weakness before pedaling away from Jan Ullrich.

2002 Armstrong dominates again with a crushing assault at the Tourmalet. The Texan's margin of victory in Paris is a huge 7 minutes and 17 seconds.

2003 In the most exciting Tour in years, Lance Armstrong and Jan Ullrich engage in a classic duel. It is also the fastest Tour ever, with the yellow jersey clocking an average speed of 40.94 kilometers per hour. Tyler Hamilton, racing with a broken collarbone, emerges as a star, winning a stage and finishing fourth. Richard Virenque ties a record with his sixth polka dot jersey.

2004 Marco Pantani, 34-year-old winner of the 1998 tour, is found dead on February 14 in a hotel room in Rimini, Italy. Drug use is implicated.

2004 Lance Armstrong and U.S. Postal absolutely dominate an unusually configured Tour de France, giving the Texan his sixth yellow jersey—and the all-time record for number of Tour wins. Jan Ullrich finishes a disappointing fourth.

2004 Tyler Hamilton wins the gold medal in road cycling at the Athens Olympics; just a few weeks later, he's accused of taking illegal blood transfusions. As of this writing, Hamilton's case was still undecided. If convicted, the rider faces a two-year ban.

Glossary: 20 Essential Terms

Arrivée: The finish line.

Autobus: The group of riders, who, in the mountains, stick together in order to help each other climb. Many of these are sprint specialists with few ascending skills, so they work together in order to avoid being eliminated from the race for finishing beyond the day's specified time limit.

Breakaway (in French, *échappée*): When a group of riders splits off from the front pack, attempting to take the lead and win the race.

Col: Mountain pass.

Caravane Publicitaire: Also known as "the Caravan." The five-mile-long parade of wildly-decorated sponsor vehicles that precedes the race; fans crowd around them to receive free product samples.

Commissaires: Tour officials. They travel in specially marked cars and enforce the rules.

Contre-la-Montre: A time trial (French for "against the watch").

Départ: The start line.

Directeur Sportif: Team manager.

Domestique: One of the essential riders who work for the team leaders—providing a barrier against oncoming wind, as well as carrying water or food forward from the team car.

Dropped: When a rider can't keep up with the rest, and falls back, he's been dropped.

Flamme Rouge: The red flame—a triangular object, suspended above the road, that marks the race's final kilometer.

GC: General classification—the overall standings in the race. If you lead in the GC, you're in first place.

Grimpeur: French for climber.

Lanterne Rouge: The rider in last place.

Lead-Out: A specialized *domestique* who pulls a sprinter forward by riding in front of him until they near the finish line, when, using reserve energy from having avoided the wind, the sprinter shoots toward the line.

Patron: The "boss" of the pack; the top rider. For the past five years, this has been Lance Armstrong.

Peloton: The main pack of riders.

Poursuivants: A group of riders attempting to chase down the race leaders.

Tête de la Course: The head of the course—where the leaders are.

Tour de France Records

Tour Winners (Yellow Jerseys)

Year	Name	Country	Year	Name	Country
1903	M. Garin	France	1954	L. Bobet	France
1904	Cornet	France	1955	L. Bobet	France
1905	Trousselier	France	1956	Walkowiak	France
1906	R. Pottier	France	1957	Anquetil	France
1907	Petit-Breton	France	1958	Gaul	Luxembourg
1908	Petit-Breton	France	1959	Bahamontès	Spain
1909	Faber	Luxembourg	1960	Nencini	Italy
1910	Lapize	France	1961	Anquetil	France
1911	Garrigou	France	1962	Anquetil	France
1912	Defraye	Belgium	1963	Anquetil	France
1913	Thys	Belgium	1964	Anquetil	France
1914	Thys	Belgium	1965	Gimondi	Italy
1919	Lambot	Belgium	1966	Aimar	France
1920	Thys	Belgium	1967	Pingeon	France
1921	Scieur	Belgium	1968	Janssen	The Netherlands
1922	Lambot	Belgium	1969	Merckx	Belgium
1923	H. Pélissier	France	1970	Merckx	Belgium
1924	Bottecchia	Italy	1971	Merckx	Belgium
1925	Bottecchia	Italy	1972	Merckx	Belgium
1926	L. Buysse	Belgium	1973	Ocana	Spain
1927	Frantz	Luxembourg	1974	Merckx	Belgium
1928	Frantz	The Netherlands	1975	Thévenet	France
1929	Dewaele	Belgium	1976	Van Impe	Belgium
1930	Leducq	France	1977	Thévenet	France
1931	A. Magne	France	1978	Hinault	France
1932	Leducq	France	1979	Hinault	France
1933	Speicher	France	1980	Zoetemelk	The Netherlands
1934	A. Magne	France	1981	Hinault	France
1935	R. Maes	Belgium	1982	Hinault	France
1936	S. Maes	Belgium	1983	Fignon	France
1937	R. Lapébie	France	1984	Fignon	France
1938	Bartali	Italy	1985	Hinault	France
1939	S. Maes	Belgium	1986	LeMond	USA
1947	Robic	France	1987	Roche	Ireland
1948	Bartali	Italy	1988	Delgado	Spain
1949	F. Coppi	Italy	1989	LeMond	USA
1950	Kubler	Switzerland	1990	LeMond	USA
1951	Koblet	Switzerland	1991	Indurain	Spain
1952	F. Coppi	Italy	1992	Indurain	Spain
1953	L. Bobet	France	1993	Indurain	Spain

Year	Name	Country
1994	Indurain	Spain
1995	Indurain	Spain
1996	Riis	Denmark
1997	Ullrich	Germany
1998	Pantani	Italy
1999	Armstrong	USA
2000	Armstrong	USA
2001	Armstrong	USA
2002	Armstrong	USA
2003	Armstrong	USA
2004	Armstrong	USA

Most Days Wearing the Yellow Jersey

96 days: Merckx
78 days: Hinault
60 days: Indurain
51 days: Anquetil

Sprinters (Green Jerseys)

Year	Name	Country	Year	Name	Country
1953	Schaer	Switzerland	1979	Hinault	France
1954	Kubler	Switzerland	1980	Pevenage	Belgium
1955	Ockers	Belgium	1981	Maertens	Belgium
1956	Ockers	Belgium	1982	Kelly	Ireland
1957	Forestier	France	1983	Kelly	Ireland
1958	Graczyck	France	1984	Hoste	Belgium
1959	Darrigade	France	1985	Kelly	Ireland
1960	Graczyck	France	1986	Vanderaerden	Belgium
1961	Darrigade	France	1987	Van Poppel	The Netherlands
1962	Altig	Germany	1988	Eddy Planckaert	Belgium
1963	Van Looy	Belgium	1989	Kelly	Ireland
1964	Janssen	The Netherlands	1990	Ludwig	Germany
1965	Janssen	The Netherlands	1991	Abdoujaparov	USSR
1966	Willy Planckaert	Belgium	1992	Jalabert	France
1967	Janssen	The Netherlands	1993	Abdoujaparov	Uzbekistan
1968	Bitossi	Italy	1994	Abdoujaparov	Uzbekistan
1969	Merckx	Belgium	1995	Jalabert	France
1970	Godefroot	Belgium	1996	Zabel	Germany
1971	Merckx	Belgium	1997	Zabel	Germany
1972	Merckx	Belgium	1998	Zabel	Germany
1973	Van Springel	Belgium	1999	Zabel	Germany
1974	Sercu	Belgium	2000	Zabel	Germany
1975	Van Linden	Belgium	2001	Zabel	Germany
1976	Maertens	Belgium	2002	McEwen	Australia
1977	Esclassan	France	2003	Baden Cooke	Australia
1978	Maertens	Belgium	2004	McEwen	Australia

King of the Mountains (Polka Dot Jerseys)

Year	Name	Country		Year	Name	Country
1933	Trueba	Spain		1972	Van Impe	Belgium
1934	Vietto	France		1973	Torres	Spain
1935	F. Vervaecke	Belgium		1974	Perurena	Spain
1936	Berrendero	Spain		1975	Van Impe	Belgium
1937	F. Vervaecke	Belgium		1976	Bellini	Italy
1938	Bartali	Italy		1977	Van Impe	Belgium
1939	S. Maes	Belgium		1978	Martinez	France
1947	Brambilla	Italy		1979	Battaglin	Italy
1948	Bartali	Italy		1980	Martin	France
1949	Coppi	Italy		1981	Van Impe	Belgium
1950	Bobet	France		1982	Vallet	France
1951	Geminiani	France		1983	Van Impe	Belgium
1952	Coppi	Italy		1984	Millar	Great Britain
1953	Lorono	Spain		1985	Herrera	Colombia
1954	Bahamontes	Spain		1986	Hinault	France
1955	Gaul	Luxembourg		1987	Herrera	Colombia
1956	Gaul	Luxembourg		1988	Rooks	The Netherlands
1957	Nencini	Italy		1989	Theunisse	The Netherlands
1958	Bahamontes	Spain		1990	Claveyrolat	France
1959	Bahamontes	Spain		1991	Chiappucci	Italy
1960	Massignan	Italy		1992	Chiappucci	Italy
1961	Massignan	Italy		1993	Rominger	Switzerland
1962	Bahamontes	Spain		1994	Virenque	France
1963	Bahamontes	Spain		1995	Virenque	France
1964	Bahamontes	Spain		1996	Virenque	France
1965	Jimenez	Spain		1997	Virenque	France
1966	Jiminez	Spain		1998	Rinero	France
1967	Jiminez	Spain		1999	Virenque	France
1968	Gonzalez	Spain		2000	Botero	Colombia
1969	Merckx	Belgium		2001	Jalabert	France
1970	Merckx	Belgium		2002	Jalabert	France
1971	Van Impe	Belgium		2003	Virenque	France
				2004	Virenque	France

Wins By Country

France	36 victories		Switzerland	2 victories
Belgium	18 victories		The Netherlands	2 victories
Italy	9 victories		Ireland	1 victory
Spain	8 victories		Denmark	1 victory
United States	9 victories		Germany	1 victory
Luxembourg	4 victories			

Multiple Individual Winners

6 victories

Lance Armstrong

5 victories

Jacques Anquetil

Bernard Hinault

Miguel Indurain

Eddy Merckx

3 victories

Louison Bobet

Greg LeMond

Philippe Thys

2 victories

Gino Bartali

Ottavio Bottecchia

Fausto Coppi

Laurent Fignon

Nicolas Frantz

Firmin Lambot

André Leducq

Sylvere Maes

Antonin Magne

Lucien Petit-Breton

Bernard Thévenet

Fastest Stage

Mario Cipollini	50.355 km/h	1999
Johan Bruyneel	49.417 km/h	1993
Adri Van Der Poel	48.927 km/h	1988
Tom Steels	48.764 km/h	1998
Patrick Sercu	48.677 km/h	1977

Fastest Time Trials

Greg LeMond	54.545 km/h	1989
Lance Armstrong	53.986 km/h	2000
Miguel Indurain	52.349 km/h	1992
Miguel Indurain	50.539 km/h	1994
Tony Rominger	50.495 km/h	1993

Most Stage Wins

Eddy Merckx (Belgium) 34

Bernard Hinault (France) 28

André Leducq (France) 25

André Darrigade (France) 22

Nicolas Frantz (Luxembourg) 20

Most Tours Participated In

Joop Zoetemelk (The Netherlands, 16)
    1970–1973, 1975–1986 (finished all)

Lucien Van Impe (Belgium, 15)
    1969–1981, 1983, 1985 (finished all)

Guy Nulens (Belgium, 15)
    1980–1994 (quit twice)

André Darrigade (France, 14)
    1953–1966 (quit once)

Raymond Poulidor (France, 14)
    1962–1970, 1972–1976 (quit twice)

Bike Brands with the Most Yellow Jersey Wins

Alcyon, France	7 wins (all pre-war)
Eddy Merckx, Belgium	5 wins (all postwar, all Merckx)
Gitane, France	9 wins (all postwar)
Peugeot, France	10 wins (7 pre-war)
Pinarello, Italy	7 wins (all postwar)
Trek, USA	6 wins (all postwar, all Armstrong)

The statistics are drawn from: Augendre, Jacques, *Guide Historique et Culturel du Tour de France, 1903–2003*, Issey-les-Moulineux, France: Amaury Sport Organization, 2003.

Bibliography

————. *The Official Tour de France: Centennial 1903–2003.* London: Weidenfeld & Nicholson, 2003.

Armstrong, Lance and Jenkins, Sally. *It's Not About the Bike: My Journey Back to Life.* New York: Putnam, 2000.

Augendre, Jacques. *Tour de France 2001.* Paris: Solar, 2001.

————. *Guide Historique et Culturel du Tour de France 1903–2003.* Issy-les-Moulineaux, France: Amaury Sport Organization, 2003.

Brunel, Philippe. *Le Tour de France Intime.* Paris: Calmann-Levy, 1995.

Dillon, Sally, et al. *Cycling France.* Victoria, Australia: Lonely Planet, 2001.

Fife, Graeme. *Tour de France: The History, The Legend, The Riders.* London: Mainstream, 1999.

Ollivier, Jean-Paul. *The Giants of Cycling.* Boulder, CO: Velo Press, 2002.

Roll, Bob. *Bobke II.* Boulder, CO: Velo Press, 2003.

Startt, James. *Tour de France/Tour de Force.* San Francisco: Chronicle Books, 2003.

Wilcockson, John, ed. *The 2003 Tour de France.* Boulder, CO: Velo Press, 2003.

In addition, the following Web sites provided invaluable statistical and historical information about the Tour:

www.backroads.com
www.bicycling.com
www.campyonly.com
www.cyclingnews.com
http//: jimlangley.com
www.lancearmstrong.com
www.letour.fr
http//:news.bbc.co.uk/sport1/hi/ other_sports/cycling/default.stm

www.memoire-du-cyclisme.net
www.torelli.com
www.tourdefrancenews.com
www.trekbikes.com
www.veloarchive.com
www.wikipedia.org

As well as these print publications:

Bicycling magazine (U.S.), *Cycle Sport* (U.K.), *L'Equipe* (France), *Pro Cycling* (U.K.), *Ride Cycling Review* (Australia), *The International Herald Tribune* (France), *The New Yorker* (U.S.), *VeloNews* (U.S.)

About the Authors

Bob Roll is imprisoned by a dark and chaotic landscape—his own mind. He competed in bicycle races, including the Tour de France, in a style all his own. He was rarely seen at the front of the peloton, but from where he *was* seen, a great mixture of joy and madness emanated. There may never be another bike racer who goes so far on results so meager. Bob commentates on a variety of bicycle races, including the Tour de France, for the Outdoor Life Network.

Dan Koeppel has been writing about bikes, bike racing, and outdoor adventure for over 20 years. He has ridden all the major Alpine climbs and passes of the Tour de France, and traveled extensively on his off-road bike throughout the U.S., Mexico, and Central and South America. In 2003, Dan was inducted into the Mountain Bike Hall of Fame. He's a contributing editor at *National Geographic Adventure* and *Bicycling* magazines, and lives in Los Angeles with two cats and a minimum of six bicycles.

Photo Credits

Index